A MAN IS NOT A PLAN

SUCCESS STRATEGIES
FOR
INDEPENDENT WOMEN

Mary Grace Musuneggi

A MAN IS NOT A PLAN

SUCCESS STRATEGIES FOR INDEPENDENT WOMEN

To contact the author, Mary Grace Musuneggi, visit:

   Website .... : www.MFGplanners.com

   Email .... : MaryGrace@MFGplanners.com

To contact the publisher, inCredible Messages Press, visit www.inCredibleMessages.com

Printed in the United States of America

ISBN 978-0-9976056-1-7 paperback

ISBN 978-0-9976056-2-4 eBook

Book Coach...... : Bonnie Budzowski

Cover design.... : Bobbie Fox Fratangelo

To protect confidentiality, names and some details of the stories in this book have been changed.

DEDICATION

To Tom:

> *Grow old along with me! The best is yet to be, the last of life, for which the first was made.*
>
> ~ Robert Browning

To my son, Christopher:

> *My very reason for having a plan.*

CONTENTS

INTRODUCTION

WHY HE JUST CAN'T BE THE PLAN

WHY HE JUST CAN'T BE THE PLAN

MOST FAIRY TALES START with the words, "Once upon a time." Like most little girls, I believed in fairy tales, especially the Cinderella story. "Someday my prince would come;" someday soon my "knight in shining armor" would come on his white horse and take me away from everything dull and ordinary. Someday Prince Charming would wake me with a kiss to be part of his exciting world.

I look back now and wonder: How could I have even imagined such a dream? Where did I learn to expect my dreams to be fulfilled by some princely, magical man?

I was raised by a single-parent mother after my father died when I was 10 years old. How could I have planned on a man to build a life for me, when as a teen, I saw my mother remarry briefly only to go through a difficult divorce?

The Cinderella story lost all its promise when I also lived the same story as my mother had not too many years later. It began with the death of my first husband a few months after the birth of our only child. A second marriage, years later, ended in divorce. When Prince Charming did come, I was fifty years old and fully able to support myself and solve my own problems.

Had my mother waited for a man to make her life fulfilling, she would have been very disappointed. Because she took responsibility for herself, she led a special and exciting life. Had I waited to plan a life around a man, I would have spent most of my life accomplishing very little.

Boys, guys, and men enter our lives at various stages; many of them will add feelings, life experiences, love, and value to our lives. But because many of them will leave our lives by choice or by chance, we need to be ready to survive. We need to be ready to add feelings, life experiences, love, and value to our own lives. We need to be prepared with the skills to make our own lives complete.

Even when we find a great man who is a prince to us, it's foolish for us to expect that man to be able to meet all of our needs. No human being is in a position to do all of that. It's our own responsibility to live full lives, developing our unique gifts, enjoying each day, enriching the lives of others, and making the world a better place.

The actress, Mae West said, "You only live once, but if you do it right, once is enough."

So to all of those who dream of being Cinderella, Snow White, or Sleeping Beauty, this book is for you. It may be time to rethink that dream. Here's to your journey of becoming an independent woman who lives the life you have planned, who lives the life that is everything you want it to be.

Because, although a man can be a special part of your plan, a man is not a plan.

CHAPTER 1

IF ONLY
CINDERELLA KNEW
THE STATISTICS

And God promised men that good and obedient wives would be found in all the corners of the earth. Then He made the world round. And He laughed and laughed and laughed.

~ Source unknown

IF ONLY CINDERELLA
KNEW THE STATISTICS

B ECAUSE I AM A FINANCIAL CONSULTANT, people naturally
assume that I talk in terms of numbers, financial analysis,
investment performance, and statistics. But I rarely ever do that.
Not only because such talk can be boring, but more importantly,
because numbers change and statistics are of little value unless
they relate specifically to the people I am speaking to.

Statistics become important to us only when they become
personal, when they have something to do with things that we
care about. The whole purpose of statistics is to provide information about what the average person experiences—and can
expect. What is happening in the world to the average man or
woman? Based on this information, what reasonable expectations
can we have for our own lives? What might happen to us because
it has happened or is happening to others? How do we fit into the
group that makes up the statistics?

For example, imagine there was a statistic that said the majority of women over the age of 55 could expect to be homeless
within the next five years. If you were a woman over the age of
55, you would want to know if that statistic is credible. You would
want to know what you needed to do to prevent homelessness.

Imagine that another statistic said the majority of men under the age of 25 who work as coal miners could expect to be unemployed within the next five years. If you were that same age 55-plus woman, you probably wouldn't find this statistic of any real importance to you, unless you have a son who is 24 and is a coal miner. Otherwise, you wouldn't much care if the statistic is credible or not.

Consider this statistic: The average age of widowhood is 56 (Investment Advisor, August 2010).

I first found this statistic in 2002. Since then I have seen various other studies that say the age is 55 or 57. Regardless of the exact number, it comes as a surprise to most women that they may be widowed at such an early age, especially with the increase in life expectancy.

Now, if you happen to be 70 and have been married to the same man for 45 years, this statistic means nothing. But when at the age of 25 I went from being a wife to being a widow, from being a stay-at-home mom married to an officer in the Marine Corps, to being an unemployed single parent of a newborn, and from living in officer's housing on a military base to being homeless, this statistic became a reality for me. Some men die at 87. Some die at 25. The average age of widowhood is 56. I was a statistic.

Consider another statistic: After the death of a spouse, the average man remarries within three years; the average woman remarries within five. (About.com 2011 citing a U.S. Census Bureau Report)

Men remarry for companionship, and I think some men marry to have someone to do the dishes. Women remarry for security and often for financial reasons. The financial challenges many widows face are compelling. Some studies say that the average woman will go through her husband's entire estate within five years. The Women's Institute for Financial Education says that 1 in 4 women will be broke within three months of their husband's death.

This dismal reality might be true for one of two reasons. A woman might go through her husband's estate quickly because the husband didn't leave his widow much in the estate. It could also be that the widow did not know how to handle what she got. In any case, the idea of being part of this statistic should bring fear into the hearts of most women. And the older we become, the harder it will be to rebound from any crisis.

I remarried 13 years (well beyond the five-year average) after the death of my husband. Fortunately, I did not enter the marriage for financial reasons. Even so, my second husband and I separated and eventually divorced. Once again, I became a statistic.

Consider the statistics from The Americans for Divorce Reform:

- 45 to 50 percent of first marriages end in divorce

- 60 to 67 percent of second marriages end in divorce

- 70 to 73 percent of third marriages end in divorce

Finally, consider this summary statistic from National Center for Women and Retirement Research:

- 90 percent of all women will spend some part of their adult life on their own.

But are we ready? Based on my experience, many of us are not.

CINDERELLA ALIVE AND WELL

I have many women friends and clients whose accomplishments, intellect, and financial savvy impress me. The women range from business owners to professionals to stay-at-home moms who pursue their own goals and collaborate in or manage their own financial health.

Yet, in spite of the examples these women set and in spite of the readily available statistics, many women still leave their fate in the hands of another human being. I see these women in my office on a regular basis.

If you are thinking that while the Cinderella concept ruled in the past, today's women are more educated, informed, and independent, consider a conversation I had with a young woman we will call Kathy. The conversation went something like this:

Mary Grace:	"I see you just graduated from college?"
Kathy:	"Yes, with a Bachelor of Arts Degree."
Mary Grace:	"What kind of career will you pursue?"
Kathy:	"I am really not planning on pursuing a career. I am planning on staying at home and raising children."
Mary Grace:	"That is a terrific career that a young woman can choose when she has children. Have you given any thought to what you might do until then, or when they go off to school, or grow up and leave home?"
Kathy:	"No, as I am not planning on ever working. I am hoping to never need to. I am planning for my husband to provide me the opportunity to always stay at home."
Mary Grace:	"And if you won't have to work, what kind of plans do you have for your life? More education? Public service? Charity? Artistic endeavors?"
Kathy:	"No, not really. I am comfortable being part of my husband's plans since he will be supporting me."
Mary Grace:	"Well, okay then. But I didn't know you were married."
Kathy:	"I'm not."
Mary Grace:	"Are you engaged, or there is someone special in your life?"
Kathy:	"Not yet. But I am sure there will be."

It may sound as though this conversation took place in the 1950s. Unfortunately, I had this talk recently with a 23-year-old college graduate.

So just at the point where you think we have "come a long way, Baby," and women are making better life choices, a segment of the female population still seems to believe that women's life goals should center around the men in their lives, whether those men exist or not.

If the statistics are true, there is a good chance that Kathy will find herself responsible for her own financial position and her own well-being at some point in her life. The timespan may last years or decades.

And what if Kathy must fend for herself after her husband leaves her with no pension, no savings, and no retirement plan? What if he dies and hasn't paid off the mortgage, bought the life insurance, or handled the finances well? What if Kathy has fore-gone additional education, life experiences, and friendships while she was focusing on her man's life? Do you think she will some-how regret leaving all the planning up to the man?

Barbara Stanny, the author of *Overcoming Under Earning: A Five Step Plan to a Richer Life*, reveals why it is so important that women focus on their own financial success. Barbara's father, who was the co-founder of H&R Block, often reminded his daughter that she was set for life. She had a trust fund and her father predicted she would marry a financially successful man. Stanny did in fact marry an attorney, who drained her trust fund and then divorced her.

I hope this dooms day scenario never befalls Kathy or you. My personal story and professional experience indicate that such a fate happens to more women than you might think. Women who come to my offices are too frequently in crisis because they de-pended entirely upon a man.

I tell these all-too-real stories as cautionary tales to encourage all women, even those who long ago left Cinderella behind, to evaluate their lives and take practical steps to live abundantly in every area, whether a man is involved or not.

Cinderella After the Honeymoon

I am sure that during my conversation with Kathy, she saw herself like Cinderella, assuming that someday her prince would come. But the chance of Kathy losing her glass slipper at the king's ball is slim to none. I always think the Cinderella story ends too soon. What do you think happens years after the prince takes her off to his castle? Are they still living happily ever after?

And what if today Cinderella had made the choice to be a stay-at-home mom, like my young friend? Consider these words by Leslie Bennetts, author of *The Feminine Mistake: Are We Giving Up Too Much?*

> Women have not been told the truth about becoming stay-at-home moms. Depending on a spouse is not just a lifestyle choice, but an economic choice with potentially dire consequences. Ageism, sexism, and the Mommy Factor will work against them. Even taking three years off will cause a 37 percent cut in earnings compared to women who remain in the workforce.

Bennetts' big concern is that young women today will end up like those of the 1950s who stayed at home only to be hit by the divorce revolution and have the rugs pulled out from under them.

Even if you have been fortunate enough to meet your white knight, the probability exists that he will ride off into the sunset long before you. Sometimes by choice, and sometimes by chance. And remember, just as a frog can turn into a prince, so can a prince turn into a frog.

Even if you are one of the 10 percent who stay married until the end, being educated, emotionally-secure, independent-thinking, and financially savvy will make your spouse's job a whole lot easier—and both of your lives more enjoyable. If your man is the prince he seems to be, he will want to be sure that you can take care of yourself.

MY OWN ANTI-CINDERELLA STORY

My first husband, Ken, was killed in a car accident at the age of 25. He was an officer in the Marine Corps, assigned to a special duty station in Memphis, while I was living on base at New River, N.C. We had just had our first child and the holidays were approaching. It was unlikely that Ken would be spending them with us.

We decided that I should go to Pittsburgh, PA, (which was where our families lived), so that our son, Christopher, would be able to spend his first Christmas there. A few days before Christmas, Ken called to let me know that he could get leave and would meet me at my mother's home, where we could stay through New Year's Day. Good news, no doubt.

The night before Ken was to arrive, he called me to discuss his plans for his trip home. In those days with no cell phones or calling plans, he called "collect," meaning that we were being charged a very high rate for every minute we talked. Although Ken seemed to want to go on and on talking to me, I reminded him of what it was costing and suggested we talk about all these things when I saw him the next day.

Ken never arrived on the next day. Only a few miles away from my mother's home, the driver of a car coming in the opposite direction fell asleep at the wheel, crashing into our car and killing both himself and Ken instantly. In that same instant, my life changed forever. I was no longer a wife and stay-at-home mother living in officer's housing. I was a single parent of an infant, with no job and no place to live.

It was hard not to think about what I would have done differently if I had only known. I would have allowed our last conversation to go on forever; I would have completed a master's degree; I would have kept up my resume by having a part-time job or doing volunteer work; I would have never used a charge card that I didn't pay off monthly. I would have bought lots and lots more life insurance on Ken. I would have had a plan in case something should happen to him.

Before I became pregnant with Christopher, I had worked for a few years as a language arts teacher. When the baby came, I thought I had 18 years before I would work outside the home again. When Ken and I met with an insurance agent, I was thinking about our future together and the education needs we would have for Christopher. The farthest thing from my mind was how I would manage financially should something happen to Ken. We didn't buy nearly enough life insurance.

The experience of losing a spouse at an early age teaches important life lessons. The most important is that I would need to get up, get dressed up, and get going if I hoped to accomplish anything. It would have been easy to wallow in my sorrow and be depressed by my plight, but I came to recognize that nothing would be accomplished that way.

Life begins with getting up each day. And then getting dressed up. It is not enough to just get dressed. Everyone gets dressed. Even nudists get dressed periodically. A sweater when it is cold. But getting dressed up means looking your best, putting your best foot forward, and feeling good about who you are. Getting dressed up means you expect the day to be special.

Once you are up and dressed up, you need to get moving. Make something happen. As a language arts teacher, I had explained to my students that a noun is only a word until you add a verb to it. Only then does the noun become a sentence. And so life requires action in order to be complete.

Another life lesson was *carpe diem* (seize the day). Each day is precious, and I would need to use every moment to improve my life, the lives of my family members, and the world around me. I learned that if I didn't do what I could in the present, I may not have the opportunity to do it ever. Ken's death was that lesson learned in stereo. I would never have the opportunity to do anything with him ever again.

When Ken died, I moved back to Pittsburgh and in with my mother. The Veterans Administration education benefits paid for me to go back to school; and unlike so many women (and men) who never take advantage of that, I began working on my master's degree. Thankfully, I did have a bachelor's degree and could apply for teaching jobs. I eventually rented a small apartment and tried to start a life. Working, going to school, and raising a baby on my own would be all the more difficult if I did not have a support system. Living near family certainly would help.

But what was it that I wanted to do? I had to start somewhere, so a job seemed like a realistic place to start.

Returning to teaching was a life lesson of its own and helped me discover another important lesson: Great goals for my life require that I step out of my comfort zone.

Ken died in December, during the Christmas season, and I began to look for a new teaching job as the year got off to a fresh start. I had rejections, interviews, and offers to work as a substitute, but I needed more.

Late in the summer, I was invited to interview at a parochial school in Pittsburgh. During the interview, I discovered that the position was for an elementary school science teacher. Had I known that, I would never have taken the interview. I just wasn't a fit. I had a degree in Language Arts, and I had failed Biology in college. What kind of science teacher would I be? Obviously, I did not get the job.

But during the second week in September, I got a call from the same school, asking me how fast I could learn the elementary school's science curriculum. A teacher had quit, school was in session, and there was an emergency.

I stepped in and learned a lot in the process. I was definitely outside of my comfort zone.

More importantly, this was 1978, and the job paid a salary of $5,000 a year. It didn't take me long to figure out that if I was to improve my life for me and my son, I needed a job that paid at least $11,000 a year so I could buy a house.

I was convinced that the best way to raise Christopher was to have a house, with a yard, a swing set, and the things that two-parent families have. I quickly learned that teaching would never get me there. It was time to step out of what I knew and go after what I needed to know.

I began by going to my local bank to meet the manager to find out how to develop a financial plan that would allow me to buy a house. I also needed to open my own savings and checking accounts. I was so excited to be on my way to reaching my first goal.

But after I explained my plan to the manger, he looked at me, shaking his head and said, "Why do you want to do all of this on your own? Don't you just want to get married again? That would be your best plan."

I responded by saying that I would think about that, but since I didn't know anyone who wanted to marry me just now, I guessed I should go about getting my finances in order. Before I left the manager's office, I jokingly asked if he knew of someone I could marry. He shrugged and said he didn't, but he just assumed a nice girl like me could find someone.

The next day I went to a local car dealer and told him I wanted to buy a car. He asked me if my husband was with me. I said I wasn't married. He said, "Well you might want to think about getting married, so you would have someone to help you take care of your car." I told him I would think about that and asked if he knew anyone who might want to marry me right now. He too said, "No," of course, and so I told him I guessed I should buy a car on my own. And so I did.

A few days later, I got in my car and drove to a local employment agency. Knowing that I needed to earn at least $11,000 to pay my bills and buy a house, I thought this was a good place to start. I didn't know what kind of jobs would pay $11,000 or what kind of skills or education I would need to get this kind of job, and I was hoping they could point me in the right directions.

The employment agent told me that there were many jobs where I could eventually make $11,000. Most companies, however, didn't hire single women for those kinds of jobs. The jobs often required training, and companies were reluctant to spend the money on training women whom they assumed would leave and get married. I said I would not be doing that. After all, I didn't know anyone whom I could marry and apparently, no one else did either; after all, I had been asking around. So I needed to get a job.

The agent asked me if I could type. I answered, "Of course, I can type. Can't all women?" In response, the agent got me an interview for a sales assistant job with a very successful life insurance agent.

Talk about stepping out of my comfort zone. I knew nothing about insurance, and I could type only a few words a minute if spelling didn't count. Even so, I was the poster child for why young couples with children should buy lots of life insurance. I suggested to the life insurance agent that he could share my story with his prospects. I also told this prospective employer that, given the chance, I could do anything.

The insurance agent asked me if I planned to get married. I promised him I wouldn't if he paid me well. He offered me $9,000 a year to be his assistant. It was not enough to buy the house, but it was a start. I thought if I did a good job, I would ask for a raise in a year or two.

A Step Beyond the Cinderella Story

Before long, working in my new career became comfortable, and I was making enough to pay my rent and other bills, but I knew I needed to take another step out of my comfort zone if I was ever going to reach the goal of buying a house.

Within six months, I started to recognize that my employer wasn't doing anything that I couldn't do if I had the education and training. I had to assume that he was earning a whole lot more than $11,000 a year if he was able to pay me $9,000.

I made a decision to talk to the owner of the agency (my boss' boss, whom we will call Sam) and ask him what I needed to do to become an agent. I was aware that there were no women agents in the firm, even though the company had been in Pittsburgh for 100 years.

It was 1981, and Sam's response to my inquiry was a reflection of the times. He laughed and said, "We don't hire women as agents. The only reason a woman would want to be an agent would be to get her MRS degree."

It took me a few moments to grasp Sam's meaning. When I finally realized what he was thinking, I responded, "I don't want to get married. I want to buy a house and I need to make more money in order to do that." He tried very hard to talk me out of this career decision.

Finally, I said, "I understand your competitor across the street is hiring. Maybe I should go there."

I'd like to believe that my determination won Sam over, but chances are he was just not going to take a chance that I might succeed with his biggest competitor. As a result, I became the company's first female insurance associate.

During my first year as an agent, I only made $8,000, so I actually went backward. The following year, however, I made $11,000 and bought my first house. Today, I make something more than that. The real value of that experience, however, was learning that sometimes life requires that we step out of our comfort zone, stress our independence, take the road less traveled, and focus on the goals that will get us to where we want to be.

Had I listened to all of the men I encountered on this journey, had I seen marriage as being my only option, I would have never entered my new career and I would have never bought that first house.

When I tell this story to women today, many express shock. How could these men talk to me like this? Isn't it illegal? Could I have sued? How were they allowed to openly discriminate just because I was a woman? Well, things were certainly different back then.

But have things really changed? Today, no potential employer is allowed to ask a woman about her personal life or her marriage plans, but I know of no women today who believe that sexual bias has been obliterated in the workplace. The difference today is that even though men cannot say it, many continue to think that women are less desirable and reliable for professional jobs.

So, do other people's opinions really have to matter? Over the years, I have learned that it doesn't matter what others think about what I can't do. All that matters is what I know I can do. Many of my accomplishments have come from me being able to take steps out of my comfort zone, out of the niche in which some thought I was predetermined to live.

Even as I began to undertake typical training as an insurance agent in the 1980s, I realized that gender bias was built right into the whole profession. The assumption was that men earned and controlled all the money. None of my instructors had ever been a woman, let alone a widow. How could they know what either could accomplish?

Although it took many years, the culture began to change, and as women were becoming more independent, some firms began to see the potential of women selling insurance to women. I received and turned down various offers to work only with women because, at the time, this seemed too specialized, and women didn't yet have control of enough money to make the niche profitable. Even so, I kept my eyes open and continued to develop my skills.

At the same time, working with male prospects could be challenging. I often was asked, "Shouldn't you be home taking care of your son?"

I would answer, "I am here taking care of my son; after all, he needs food on the table and a roof over his head. That is what my career provides." I refused to give up. I had been taught that persistence was the key.

Eventually, the insurance company for which I worked started to take on financial planning clients. I knew that all women could benefit from good financial advice. I decided that my mission would be to help men and women make wise decisions with their money.

I got all the necessary licenses to work in the financial planning arena. I studied and worked to become a CLU (Chartered Life Underwriter) and a ChFC (Chartered Financial Consultant). I was working 24/7 and raising Christopher 24/7, but I considered the education and experience a "must do." I needed the credibility.

Having been an educator in my early life made the transition to being a financial educator and planner easy. Teaching both men and women how to become financially independent was right up my alley. This role gave me the opportunity to share my training, education, and my life experiences. I was able to help women learn from my own personal life challenges, changes, and circumstances.

Having found my niche, I rose to a level of success within the firm that I had never anticipated. I was doing what I loved and earning a living doing it. Isn't that the real definition of success?

Within a few years, I was eyeing the position of investment manager for the firm. The current manager was ill and planning to retire. But to get the job, I needed the approval of Sam, the man who had originally hired me merely to keep me away from his competitor across the street.

Not much had changed with Sam over the years. Even though I had reached success within the firm, his vision of what women could and couldn't do hadn't changed. Initially, he refused to even interview me, but he finally relented under pressure from my colleagues. My male colleagues who had once doubted my ability were now supportive of me.

I still remember how Sam explained his reasoning for not wanting to interview a woman:

> I didn't want you at first because I've learned that women do not put a price on their time. They just give, and give, and give it away. This job requires that you place a value on your time.

Unlike the time when I first interviewed with Sam and I felt he was wrong that women only want jobs in the business world just to get their "MRS Degree," this time I knew Sam was right. Women do just give and give their time, and often they don't realize what value they give away. In general, women don't really recognize what they trade for the time they give. But I am pretty sure even today, where I value my time much more, that giving away some of our time is how women build relationships. And there is great value in the relationships we build, both personally and professionally.

As it turned out, Sam did hire me for the position. Once again he said he would "take a chance" on me because everyone else in the firm seemed to want me in the job. He reminded me how lucky I was to get the position; and I reminded him how lucky he and the firm would be with me in the position. Sometimes you just have to sing your own praises.

So having been the first female advisor in the firm, I now became the first female investment manager in the firm. I continued to develop my skills and build a clientele, always championing independence and financial savvy for women.

Meanwhile, my son, Christopher, graduated from college and secured a job with an accounting firm. Although he enjoyed accounting while in the academic world, he realized he didn't like it in the real world. He wanted to work more with people and less with the numbers.

As fate would have it, while he was looking for a more people-oriented job, Christopher received an offer to work in the compliance department at the same firm where I worked. I thought it was interesting when Christopher accepted the job, as I would have thought he would have wanted to go elsewhere.

From the time that he was 2 years old, Christopher had "worked" with me at the firm. I would bring him into the office and he would play or nap under my desk. On weekends, he would join me to do filling in my office. Not having the resources back then to pay for staff, I did all aspects of the job on my own. But I taught him to be a very good helper. He learned ABCs long before going to kindergarten, and he understood business protocol at a very early age. So when he chose a career, I just thought he might want to do something different.

No one was more surprised than I when Christopher announced that he would like to do what I do. I was, however, proud and pleased that he would think to follow me into the business. My only stipulation was that we not live together if we worked together. Christopher got his own apartment; and then became a junior advisor working under me.

Christopher was the one who eventually suggested we start our own firm. As we began to talk, I realized that it would be cool to set our own direction and make our own rules. We made a nine-month plan for me to step down from management at our old firm and to move into our own offices.

The firm for which Christopher and I worked actually supported our plan and allowed for a smooth transition. It was an amazing twist when six months into our move, that firm and its parent company announced it was closing, after 125 years in Pittsburgh. How sad for them and their employees and for those advisors who were left behind, those who only had a few months to transition out on their own. How fortunate for us that we had made the move when we did. Christopher and I were already where we wanted to be. Once again, I realized that timing is everything. That company closed and The Musuneggi Financial Group stepped forward.

As our firm has grown, my passion for independence for women has never faltered. Experience tells me that a woman's financial independence is one aspect of a complete whole. Any woman's financial independence is inextricably linked to how she manages so many other aspects of her life—areas like relationships and health and business—especially during times of change or transition.

In 2003, Christopher and I started Single Step Strategies as a nexus of professionals and organizations who provide educational and enrichment opportunities for women in Western PA. Our goal is to empower women in our community by directing them to resources that can help them manage life's challenges and changes—one step at a time.

Everything starts with one step. One step can move you toward independence. Begin by deciding that no matter where you are in life—whether with a man or not—you will live abundantly and sow seeds of independence so that you can create the life you want now and tomorrow. This protects you if you should become a statistic, and makes good sense even if you don't.

SINGLE STEP STRATEGIES

Single Step Strategies is about identifying and taking steps toward abundant living. Abundant living means:

1. Finding Your Purpose and Living for It

   Recognize that you are a person of worth, with or without validation from a man or anyone else. You were born for a reason, and you have a unique contribution to make to the world. If you minimize yourself in order to let others shine, you cheat yourself and the world around you. There is plenty of room in life for you to develop your own abilities while caring for a family—and while being a mate, a partner, a friend, working a job, going to school, or building a career. Abundant living means being the best "you" that you can be.

2. Taking Appropriate Control of Your Life

   All relationships involve tradeoffs, but don't fall into the trap of believing your needs should always be the lower priority. Every quarter, or at least every year, set goals for your own growth and enjoyment. Celebrate and develop your unique talents and abilities. For example, if you want to get an education, make a plan to accomplish the goal in manageable steps, even if accomplishing those steps extend beyond typical timeframes. If you want to pursue an athletic challenge, make time in your schedule to do so. If you are passionate about a specific cause, volunteer your time and talents to that cause.

3. Thinking in Terms of Creativity and Quality of Life
    Figure out what gives you satisfaction, energy, and joy, and
    build those things into your life, whether the people around
    you want to come along for the ride or not. Living abundant-
    ly means you create your own definition of quality of life—
    without looking to others for approval. For example, my
    mom was a single mother who worked hard and struggled to
    pay our bills. Yet, she believed that we should have a summer
    vacation every year. Many years, we vacationed at home—
    finding something new and different to experience right
    around our home. Mom's attitude made these vacations great,
    even when the circumstances were humble.

4. Embracing Your Freedom to Choose
    We shape our lives by our choices, in the big picture and in
    mundane ways. Failing to choose or allowing others to
    choose for us is a choice in itself. We always have a choice
    about how to use our time and how to respond to the things
    that happen in our lives. We have the freedom to remove
    ourselves from toxic people and situations.

5. Seeking Out What You Need From Multiple Sources
    When Cinderella rides off with her prince, we get the impres-
    sion that every need she has will be supplied by his largesse.
    Outside of fairytales, no one person is large enough to meet
    all of our needs. We sabotage our relationships and ourselves
    when we expect too much from one person. Friendships are
    a vital part of every healthy person's life; plus, we all need
    time alone.

Chapter 2

Bad Things Happen for a Reason: Bad Choices

It is a funny thing about life; if you refuse to accept anything but the best, you very often get it.

~ Somerset Maugham

CHAPTER 2

BAD THINGS HAPPEN
FOR A REASON: BAD CHOICES

"Everything happens for a reason."
"Someday it will all make sense."
"God has a plan."

I WAS RAISED on expressions like these. Being raised by an Irish mother and schooled by the Catholic Mercy nuns, these were always the "simple" answers to life's complicated questions. I kept asking, "Why?" Life never answered.

I got double doses of such phrases after my husband died within nine months of the birth of our son. I found myself looking up to the sky and asking, "So exactly what were You thinking?" Those around me asked me to have faith, because somehow I was supposed to believe that what was supposed to happen, did happen. And I should not anticipate getting an immediate answer to life's questions.

As time went on, I did recognize that difficult life events are teaching moments, learning experiences. And so I learned, and learned, and learned. I learned there are some things I can control and lots of things I can't. I learned that when I can control life's events, I should. When I can't control life's events, I need to accept that and move on.

In moving on, establishing life goals, and working toward them, I was able to increase my sense of independence. But looking back to the times I lost my way, didn't feel capable, or got frozen in time, I see that I had ignored my common sense. I didn't trust my gut or the inner voice that tells me right from wrong. I allowed someone or something to dictate to me what to do in my life instead of using my five senses, respecting my sixth sense, and depending on my common sense. The same has often been true of women I've met over the years who are struggling financially, emotionally, or spiritually. Often the struggle was created by a pure lack of common sense.

Taking "everything happens for a reason" to a higher plane, I recently read a quote from an unknown source: "Everything happens for a reason. Some times that reason is that you act stupid and make bad choices." How true.

A few years ago, I had the opportunity to have dinner with Jack Canfield, motivational speaker and author. He is best known as the co-creator of the *Chicken Soup for the Soul* book series. Canfield expressed his belief that wherever we are in life, it is because of the choices we have made. And wherever we go from here will be the result of the choices we make going forward. We can't do anything about the choices we have already made, except to learn from the bad ones and applaud the good ones.

You may be thinking that some choices were made for you. Someone else made the decision, be it a parent, a spouse, or a boss. But in those times, you had the choice to accept the decisions that were made for you—or not.

You may be thinking that some things that happened in your life were totally out of your control. Yes, some things happen by chance or accident. Life sends a car accident, illness, death of a spouse, loss of a job, and more. In such instances, you still have a choice—not in what is happening, but in how you respond to the event.

The daily news is filled with accounts of people who have experienced horrific life changes and have risen above the problems to lead amazing lives. The amazing lives begin with the choice these individuals make in response to their experience; they make the choice to accept the challenge and live fully in the midst of it. We stand in awe of their courage.

Thankfully, most of us will never face the most horrific of life's ordeals. Our choices are more of the day-to-day, how-to-get-through-the-day, variety. But all choices on the path to living fully require courage. And all choices have consequences, even the little ones.

Understanding that we always have a choice can be empowering. Failing to understand that all choices have consequences can be life altering.

Over the years, I have met many women who have made choices both purposely or by omission that have come to seriously affect their lives. In either case, they had a choice on how to plan for their lives and didn't; or they had the ability to make a good choice on how they would react to a life issue, and chose to act "stupid" and make bad choices instead. Some learned from their mistakes. Some came to repeat them over and over again. Most of their bad choices stem from faulty assumptions, unrealistic expectations, and even a learned helplessness.

Pauline's choice can serve as an inspiration for all of us. Pauline lived happily with her partner, Denise. While they lived in the house Denise had purchased, the couple purchased furniture and art together. They traveled, entertained, and shared a sense of adventure.

Unfortunately, Denise became ill suddenly and passed away at a young age. Since Denise and Pauline had made no legal arrangements for the passing of the home or other assets, Denise's parents removed Pauline from the home and took ownership of everything inside.

Pauline, in the face of a tragic circumstance, had a choice to make. She could fight, resent, and burn with anger as well as grief. Instead, she chose to accept the situation and move on with her life. Pauline purchased a home of her own and continues traveling, entertaining, and doing the things she enjoyed.

Pauline certainly learned from this experience and will make better plans in the future. However, at the same time, she made the life-affirming choice to let go of past mistakes rather than let them ruin how she lives today.

We all need to align our choices with outcomes we desire—walking on the path of living life to the fullest, whatever our circumstances. We do have power to shape our own lives, but it will only happen if we take control. We have to stop believing that any other individual is here to be our plan. We are the architects of our own life's plan.

But Won't He Take Care of Me?

Married for 25 years, Beth was now going through a divorce. With little financial knowledge, she was intimidated by any financial discussion.

Beth had left all the financial decisions up to her husband during their marriage, even though he had managed to have them file bankruptcy twice during that time. She continued to allow him to handle their finances, even while the divorce process was going on. Perhaps without ever being fully conscious of her choice, Beth chose to omit learning about, or participating in, financial matters in her home. She failed to summon the courage to face her financial fears.

Karen had spent many years in a physically abusive marriage. As happens in many of these marriages, her husband controlled all the money. Control is the very basis of abuse—the foundation that allows it to continue. And lack of money stops the pathway out.

Karen's husband filed all the tax returns, not allowing Karen to help complete or even review the forms—but only to sign them. Years later, after Karen was finally free of the marriage and just getting on her feet financially, she got a notice from the IRS that much of the information on the returns was fraudulent. At the time her ex-husband was not working. So when the IRS came back with fines and penalties, they came after Karen and garnished her wages. It took her many years to unravel and recover from all of this.

Thankfully, Karen found the courage to take control of her own life. First, she managed to disentangle herself from an abusive spouse and, when the need arose, she hired an accountant and took control of her own financial affairs.

Anita is another woman who chose to allow her husband to control her affairs. I met Anita years ago when I first got into business and was looking for a housekeeper. A number of women came for an interview, but Anita is the one I remember. She came to the door looking tired and disheveled, dragging two small children behind her. She said she really needed the job, as her husband had just passed away. She had felt fortunate not to have to work outside the home while her husband was alive, but this "good fortune" had a dark side. It accounted for why Anita had no skills or job experience.

When I asked if her husband had made any financial arrangements for her in the event of his death, Anita answered, "Obviously not. And you think he would have. He spent his life teaching other people to do that."

"What was his occupation?" I asked.

Anita answered, "He was an insurance agent."

Ouch, I could feel the ache in my heart.

Beth, Karen, and Anita all made choices based on unrealistic assumptions. I don't judge them for their choices, but I do want to point them out.

Beth assumed that she would have a lifetime marriage and that she could trust her husband to take care of her financially. She assumed this dependent relationship would make her happy. Based on these assumptions, Beth made a choice of omission and failed to learn how to manage money on her own.

Karen, at least for some time, stayed with a controlling, abusive husband. She chose to sign the tax forms he gave to her, assuming she could trust him to complete those forms legally.

While she was able to free herself from that toxic relationship, she paid a high price for the choice to sign those forms.

Anita assumed that her insurance salesman husband would use his knowledge and skills to provide for her and her children. Based on that assumption, she made a choice to leave insurance decisions up to him. Her choice not to be involved in financial decisions—or even stay informed of them—left her and her children destitute when her husband died.

But It Will Never Happen to Me

When my first husband, Ken, and I were newly married, we were approached by a number of insurance agents about buying a life insurance plan. Because Ken was in the Marine Corps, we had some insurance through the military. We decided that we were educated, employable, and able to take care of ourselves if the need arose. Not necessarily true, but it was what we believed. So we didn't buy.

Once I became pregnant, the whole discussion changed. We realized that if something happened, one of us would have to raise a child on his or her own. When the next insurance agent walked through the door, we bought. But we assumed we would never use the insurance, and we made a choice based on that assumption. We thought we would eventually use the plan we bought to provide additional retirement income. So we bought the expensive type of insurance that would build cash for the future.

Who would know that just nine months later, Ken would be gone and I would be a single parent? When the insurance proceeds arrived, I was grateful, but I wished we had bought a thousand times more. And instead of buying insurance that might help with retirement, we should have bought tons of inexpensive term insurance that would have paid to buy a house, funded Christopher's education, and provided an additional source of income.

While participating with Ken in our insurance decisions, I still made a choice based on a faulty assumption. Ken and I both thought the worst couldn't happen to us. When the worst did happen, I paid the price for our unrealistic choice.

BUT I WAS RAISED THIS WAY

Marissa and Lily were sisters whose father believed that girls should graduate from high school and then get married. He saved to send his two sons to college, but the two daughters were expected to work at low-paying jobs until their prince came, married them, and promised to take care of them for the rest of their lives. Having been raised this way, and having a mother who never worked outside the home, they had no reason to believe anything else.

As it turned out, Marissa became pregnant when she was relatively young and married the father of her child. Initially being unsure that she should marry this particular man, Marissa thought about raising the baby on her own. But that same father, who thought she didn't need an education, convinced her that the only honorable choice was to marry the baby's father.

It did not matter that the baby's father wasn't a particularly honorable person and did not want to get married either. He didn't want children. In fact, on the day of their wedding, after the service and during the reception, he went off with a group of women for a joy ride in his Mustang. Marissa was not one of those women.

The idealized concepts of decency, honor, and maturity that Marissa's father insisted upon moved Marissa to marry the father of her child. But the man she married possessed none of these qualities. After all, without skills and without family support, she didn't see another choice. Marissa married a man who mistreated her and her child. She divorced him two years later. Her father's plans for her didn't match her reality.

The marriage and the divorce were a crisis, but Marissa learned from her experience and used it as an opportunity to make a new choice, one that allowed her to be independent and create a life of her own. She went to nursing school, graduated, and created a healthy life for her and her child.

In the meantime, while her brothers were going to college, Marissa's sister, Lily, was also participating in another dependent "girl" saga. At a very young age, Lily married an older entrepreneur. Unlike Marissa, her sister's marriage was filled with love. But unfortunately, her husband passed away of cancer early in their marriage. At the time of his death, they had a daughter who was two years old. Their son was born three months after his father's death.

Due to some complicated finances and poor estate planning, Lily had financial difficulties. She had no education, had not pursued interests of her own, and had chosen not to participate in—or be informed of—the financial decisions of the family. Lily had entered marriage young and dependent

Unlike her sister, Lily continued to accept her father's concept that her success and happiness depended on a man's care and protection. Lily felt lonely, isolated, and lost. She began to search for someone to fill her void.

One night, while attending a dance at a local club, she met a man named Karl. He was tall and good looking and loved to dance. As did she. She had a great time.

For six months, Lily and Karl met two evenings a week to dance. She wanted the relationship to go forward. Over time, Lily recognized that she and Karl never went dancing on the weekends and they never met on holidays. Karl did not want to join Lily for group outings or double dates. Still, Lily refused to see the obvious issue, one that all of her friends knew.

When Lily was pressed by her friends to force the issue, she asked Karl if he was married. Karl told Lily that he and his wife were separated. She never pressed him for more information, and he never volunteered.

Lily made the choice to avoid the truth because it was easier than thinking about how lonely she would be once again if Karl stopped seeing her. She failed to summon the courage to face her reality.

The tide turned when Valentine's Day arrived, and Karl told her he had to work late that night. Lily knew the time had come to ferret out the truth. She waited in her car outside Karl's office and followed him to his home, only to watch him exit his house dressed up and escorting a person who could only be his wife.

Lily was traumatized. The next day, Lily called to confront Karl. He told her that he was still married and intended to divorce his wife in order to be with Lily. But he just couldn't tell his wife he was leaving her on Valentine's Day.

While there are women who would accept this explanation, Lily wasn't one of them. She hung up the phone and made the choice never to see Karl again. She couldn't help but think that if Karl cheated on his current wife, he would likely cheat on her if she became wife number two. She had finally summoned the courage to stand on her self-respect. But the hurt that came with this decision affected Lily for a long time.

Marissa and Lily were both hurt by the sexist views imposed upon them by their father. In teaching them to expect a man to come and take care of them for life, he created an unrealistic expectation. This, along with his refusal to provide a post high school education or training for his daughters, set the young women up for bad choices and dependence.

Once the sisters were out from under their father's thumb, however, they had the chance to make their own choices, both small and big. Within their marriages, they had choices and opportunities to build some independence. They certainly had choices when their marriages ended.

BUT I DON'T WANT TO BE ALONE

Angela was the quintessential administrative assistant. She was bright, attractive, talented, goal-oriented, well educated, and highly skilled. When it came to relationships, however, her self-confidence was abysmally low. Angela was insecure and convinced that the male counterparts in her relationships never cared as much about her as she did about them.

One relationship after another didn't work out. This only reinforced Angela's fears and insecurities. Then she began to find herself attracted to married men.

One such man was her boss, Frank. It's unclear how this relationship worked for her, when relationships with single men never did. Perhaps knowing her "competition" allowed Angela to know where she stood with this man.

Frank made it clear from the beginning that he did not intend to leave his wife and four children. As years went on, Frank kept that commitment to his family even as he developed a different kind of commitment to Angela.

Frank bought Angela a house, a car, and clothes. He paid many of her bills so that she could enjoy a higher level of lifestyle than her salary afforded. He took her on trips. Angela seemed content with this arrangement, even though Frank was never with her on holidays, never really took her out in public, and was not available when she was ill or needed emotional support.

What made such a relationship acceptable to Angela? She had years of opportunities to make a different choice, to pursue a relationship in which she was not second fiddle, the low-priority "wife." She also had enough skills to be independent, to rely on herself.

Angela seems to have bought into the assumption that the love of a man was of the highest importance. This male love was so important that Angela sacrificed her self-respect to obtain a reduced share. It seems her insecurities were so deep that she couldn't find the courage to insist on being treated with the respect every woman deserves.

One day Angela arrived at work, only to discover that Frank had died the night before. Being the other woman, no one had called her to let her know, and she could not attend the funeral. With Frank's death went the income that paid for Angela's house, car, and lifestyle. Angela's choices had created her circumstance.

But Angela was not the only woman in this scenario. Greta was Frank's wife.

About 20 years into their relationship, after their children were grown, Greta had admitted that she had been fully aware of the relationship Frank had with Angela all along. When Angela had learned that Greta knew, her hopes soared that Frank might leave his wife and marry her. As it turned out, Greta did not intend to ask for a divorce, and Frank was fine with that.

It seems that the financial security Frank provided Greta and her children was of ultimate importance to her. She chose to stay married to an unfaithful husband as a trade-off for financial security.

But why do some women make the assumption that financial security is only possible in having a relationship to a man? Why do women live with continuing betrayal in order to have security? Why do they fail to look around and see that countless women are supporting themselves? Why do they fail to find the courage that they need to be capable of making a life for themselves and their children?

CELEBRITIES AND CITY WOMEN

Recently, yet another famous female celebrity died of alcohol and drug abuse. It seems she found solace in a substance addiction while in a relationship with a "bad boy." In fact, it seems the celebrity in question was addicted to the bad boy. At the height of her career, she got involved with a bad boy who abused her, used her, and brought her down. She did not choose to leave—and she paid with her life for that choice.

Only a few days ago in our city, a young woman died at the hands of her husband. Her friends and family said they were not surprised that he was the responsible party. You see, she had put out a protection of abuse order against him when they were engaged. Before they got married, this woman's fiancé had pushed her down a flight of steps.

From a distance, we ask ourselves: Why would a woman marry a man who has already demonstrated that he is abusive? Why do women stay with abusive men? Why do some women seek out the "bad boy?" The assumption behind this choice differs from the ones we've been discussing so far. Rather than assume a man should rescue them, women who seek out bad boys may be seeking to be the rescuer.

According to Rabbi Shmuley Boteach, author and talk show host on Oprah Radio, women date the bad boys because they think the bad boy needs rescuing. Rabbi Boteach explains that "some women have a messiah complex—they want to be the person who can rescue the bad boy."

Such women think they are the only one to recognize the diamond in the rough in the bad boy. They reason, "Everyone else sees him as a bad boy, but I know the tender heart he has."

Boteach says, "When you are the only one who can rescue the guy, you're special, unique. You immediately have a special relationship with him that no other woman has because only you can help him."

Countless women define themselves and define their own self-worth based on the role they play in relation to a man. If they can fix the bad boy, they can believe they are an important person.

Grade School and Grown-up Girls: My Funny Valentine

Do you remember preparing for Valentine's Day in elementary school? Did you carefully decorate your shoebox, write out your cards, and choose the best card for that "someone special" whom you liked so much?

Did you watch as your dreamy "someone special" walked past your desk to give his "someone special" card to that overly-adorable, sickeningly-sweet, teacher's-pet little girl, who wouldn't give him the time of day? It was enough to make you scream.

By the end of the school day on Valentine's Day, did you allow the number, size, and shape of the cards you received to define you as popular—or not; in the right clique—or not; worthy of love—or not? If so, you are in good company. Who didn't determine her self-worth based on these judgments? We were kids raised on fantasy, and we didn't know any better.

Here's the problem: 20, 30, 40 years later, not much has changed, especially around holidays. We still want to be Cinderella, especially on Valentine's Day. If we can't be swept away by Prince Charming, we want to be the one who gets the "special someone" valentines.

We define ourselves as single, divorced, widowed, happily attached, sadly unattached, or in the wrong relationship with the wrong person. Many of us feel less than whole because we live with the guy who will never think to buy us flowers and candy—but he might get our car washed for us.

For many of us, it doesn't matter what we accomplish at work or in the community. It doesn't matter that we juggle our children and household responsibilities until we fall exhausted into bed each night. We still define our own self-worth based on the attention and romantic gestures we receive from a man. We can thank Disney's *Cinderella* and Julia Roberts' *Pretty Woman* for that.

Or can we? Isn't it our job to grow up from grade school girls to mature women? At some point, it becomes our responsibility to adjust our expectations from fairy tales to life in the real world. When we fail to do this, we self-sabotage and pay high prices.

WHAT ABOUT YOU: WHAT CHOICES ARE YOU MAKING?

You may have found reflections of your own story in one or more of the stories in this chapter. Maybe you've been grateful that your own situation or choices aren't so extreme.

Either way, you have to face the truth about yourself. Each of us has made some poor choices, some of which have lingering consequences. Each of us has also made good choices that we can celebrate.

To make sure the good choices win the day from here forward, you need to examine the assumptions you hold—and to examine how those assumptions drive your choices. It's time to examine how those choices are either expanding or contracting your life.

It's time to move from fantasy to maturity and begin stepping into the life you want for yourself. It may seem like a monumental task, one that takes more courage than you have, but it's the only path to an abundant life. As always, the choice is yours. As always, you can take one step at a time.

For now, reflect on your answers to the following questions:

1. What did your parents teach you (deliberately, by example, or by fairytale) to expect in a relationship with a man? How does this match with reality?

2. What percentage of your own definition of self-worth is based on approval from others (including spouse, parents, boss, and/or community)? In other words, what percentage of your life is determined by other people's ideas of what you should do?

3. What percentage of your own definition of self-worth is based on a fairy-tale concept of romantic love?

4. How much of your own definition of self-worth is based on your own skills, accomplishments, and worthiness as a unique human being?

5. How might you live differently if you stopped "needing" the approval of others?

6. If the worst should happen to your spouse or partner, how ready would you be to stand on your own?

7. What choices of omission are you making because you haven't found the courage to learn or do something that frightens you? For example, are you afraid to learn about finances, prepare for a career, make a career move, or buy your own car?

CHAPTER 3

THE PATH

Never put the keys to your happiness in someone else's pocket.

~ Source unkown

CHAPTER 3

THE PATH

A CLIENT NAMED Michelle once told me that she did not consider herself happily married, but she did think she had a *good* marriage. She explained, "Unlike some husbands, mine brings home his paycheck, loves the kids, never steals from me, and doesn't hit me."

Hearing Michelle's view of a good marriage stopped me in my tracks. Her criteria seemed awfully low to me. The conversation also reminded me of how easy it is to fall into the trap of assuming that whatever relationship we have is the best we can expect.

In the busy days of fulfilling our responsibilities with home, kids, work, and community, we fail to stop and think about our own criteria for a "good" love relationship. If we had clear criteria in mind at the start of the relationship, we might fail to see the relationship deteriorate once we wear a wedding ring or live in the same house.

When the opportunity arises, I ask family therapists to describe the necessary criteria for a good relationship. The professionals mention trust, security, and making room for the other person to learn and grow. They talk of demonstrating support for each other's goals and putting your partner's needs ahead of your own. Therapists say good relationships have good communication. They say healthy relationships are ones in which each partner feels a sense of freedom and independence.

When a relationship is one-sided, it is not a relationship at all. It might be one person controlling another—or one person depending upon another—or one person choosing to be subservient to the other.

I recently saw a news segment on the topic of toxic relationships that listed Dr. Greg Popcak's five signs that indicate a person is in a toxic relationship. Soon after, I read an article by Yvette Bowlin, published on the website *Tiny Buddha*, naming the same five signs. Clearly, some recognizable signs can let us know if we are in the wrong relationship for the wrong reason.

We might initially think that a toxic relationship must include physical abuse, cheating, or name-calling. According to the experts, this is not necessarily so. Toxic relationships manifest themselves in internal turmoil, even when no external bruising is involved. Here is a paraphrase of Brown's five signs of a toxic relationship:

1. It seems you can't do anything right. The other person constantly puts you down.

2. Everything is about the other person and never about you. Your feelings are neither valued nor respected.

3. You find yourself unable to enjoy good moments with the other person. You always feel criticized.

4. You're uncomfortable being yourself around the other person. You don't feel free to speak your mind. You barely recognize yourself in this person's presence.

5. You feel constricted rather than allowed to grow and change. The other person seems to think you will always be the person you are today. The other person may mock your efforts to change.

For more discussion on the above, see
http://tinybuddha.com/blog/5-signs-youre-in-a-toxic-relationship/

You know you are in a toxic relationship when you feel less and less like yourself—and more and more like you are compromising your goals and denying what is natural for you. Brown describes toxic as "something that drains life and energy."

I think of my client, Michelle, who said her husband doesn't beat her or steal from her. There are days when she hates to go home, doesn't even want to be in her own house. Her husband may not be beating her, but he certainly is a presence that drains her life and energy.

Michelle's husband is not helping her to live a full life and become all that she can be. Hers is not the relationship of anyone's dreams. It may be unrealistic to hope for Cinderella's Prince Charming, but is this the best Michelle can hope for?

Whatever our situation in life, we need to step back regularly and take stock of the quality of our love relationships. We might ask questions like these:

1. What's my definition of a good marriage/relationship?
2. What's my definition of a full life?
3. What limits does my marriage/relationship place on my dreams and ambitions? Are these limits reasonable?
4. What limits do I place on my dreams and ambitions?
5. Have I identified and communicated my dreams and ambitions to my partner? Have I asked for support?
6. What fears and/or role expectations keep me from living the life I want? Am I hiding behind my kids, my family, my job, etc.?
7. If I am unhappy in my relationship, what responsibilities do I have to make a change?
8. Under what conditions is a relationship no longer acceptable?
9. If I should need to stand on my own tomorrow, by choice, chance, or circumstance, would I be ready?

You might react in a number of ways as you think through these questions. For example, you might conclude that your relationship is toxic—and irreparable. In order to be healthy, you might have to leave the relationship.

On the other hand, you might conclude that your relationship is okay, except for one or two important areas. If so, you will have to decide if repair is possible—and if the relationship is worth your effort to work toward change.

Then again, you might conclude that your relationship is good, but your life is still not the full and rich one you desire. You might have dreams that are stalled but not lost. You will have to decide how much you want those dreams.

Finally, you might conclude that your relationship is great. If so, you will have reason to be grateful. Chances are you will still find ways to improve your relationship and your life.

Wherever you find yourself, achieving your fullest life (inside or outside of a romantic relationship) will require honesty and courage. It will also require change. Perhaps the fundamental question is this: How much change do you need to live the life of your dreams?

CHANGE ... NOT SO EASY

A man once lived with his dog in a house with a big front porch. Every morning, the dog would go outside and lie on the porch. For the entire time he was there, the dog would whine. Eventually the owner would call him and the dog would go inside.

After some months, the man's neighbors became weary of the whining. A group of them approached the owner and demanded he find out what was causing the dog to whine and put a stop to it. Was the dog ill? Was he sad? Was he in pain?

In response to their confrontation, the dog owner explained that on the spot where the dog lay was a nail. As the dog lay on the porch, the nail irritated him, and that was the source of the whining.

The neighbors, taken aback, asked the owner, "Why doesn't the dog just get up and move from the spot?"

The owner replied, "Sometimes putting up with the pain of what you know is easier than suffering through the pain of having to change."

How many of us put up with the pain of an unhappy life or a bad relationship because we believe it is easier to deal with the pain we know than suffer the pain of trying to change?

The choices we made in the past have brought us to where we are today. If we are not where we had hoped to be, then we made the wrong choices. If so, the first choice we have to make now is the choice to change. Like the dog, we will never end the pain unless we get up and move.

You may be saying, "Why didn't the owner just remove the nail?" The owner could have done that, and maybe he should have. But he didn't. Perhaps you are waiting for someone to come along and initiate a change for you. What if that someone never comes?

Happiness is a choice. You have to make it. No one can make that choice for you.

I have heard people say, "I will do things differently when the kids grow up, when I get that promotion, when I hit the lottery." These people are always waiting for some indistinct future . . . and not making the decision to change their world "now."

Jim Rohnn, in a piece called "Change Begins with Choice," reminds us:

> If you don't like how things are—change it! You are not a tree. You are not stuck in one place. You have the ability to move and to totally change every area in your life—and it all begins with your very own power of choice.

CHANGING TO A GOOD RELATIONSHIP

At least as a beginning, it seems reasonable to expect a good relationship to feature the opposite of the five signs of a toxic relationship. The signs of a good relationship might look something like this:

1. The other person expresses belief in your competence. You feel affirmed more often than criticized.

2. Your relationship is a partnership in which each person is equally important. In the complexity of life, your relationship is like a dance in which sometimes one partner is at center stage, and sometimes the other partner is at center stage. Both partners feel valued and respected.

3. You enjoy good moments with this person. Although everything isn't always wine and roses, being together is generally an affirming and uplifting experience.

4. You feel like your authentic self around this other person. You don't feel compelled to play a role or censure yourself.

5. Your relationship is one in which each partner grows and changes. The growth and change may take many forms, including formal or informal schooling or certifications, learning projects, hobbies, friendships, adventures, volunteerism, and more.

Each relationship is unique, and the outward appearance of one healthy relationship will not be the same as the outward appearance of another. It's a positive inner sense of self that counts.

Just as a toxic relationship is characterized by inner turmoil, a good relationship is characterized by the sense that your authentic self is loved and affirmed. In a good relationship, you feel comfortable in your own skin and your own home. This doesn't mean you and your spouse never fight or get irritated with one another; just that the overriding sense is a positive one.

A marriage or long-term relationship, at its best, consists of two individuals who strive to help each other reach their fullest potential—but it is more than that. While a good relationship has intrinsic value for the couple involved, the entity created by that couple has a broader purpose.

The partnership creates something bigger than the sum of its parts. Depending on the relationship, the bigger things might be children, a business, community service, an artistic contribution, or anything else.

A measure of the satisfaction in any relationship is the bigger things you create together. On days when all the children are sick or the business is struggling, you may not feel the bigger purpose, but it undergirds you nonetheless. In the face of life's changes, purpose is an anchor.

A good relationship has a firm anchor, but that doesn't mean it is static. As individuals, we change as we move through the changes in life. To be healthy, we must change as couples too.

The priorities we have in our earliest years of establishing a career may be different from the priorities we have when parenting elementary school children. These priorities, in turn, may be different from the ones we have in middle age or our retirement years. The expectations we have change as we age.

In a healthy life, we are growing as well as changing throughout our lives. In a healthy relationship, we are growing as individuals—and we are growing together as a couple. This is the only way the marriage, the relationship, the partnership is sustainable—and it doesn't happen automatically. A good relationship requires maintenance. In all relationships, we either grow together or grow apart.

ASSUMPTIONS, EXPECTATIONS, AND COMMUNICATION

If you find your relationship falls short of ideal and you want to improve it, you may have some work to do. The first step is to look inward, at your own role in the relationship.

Donna Billings was surprised to discover that her own assumptions were responsible for a significant portion of the constriction she felt in her marriage.

Donna describes her journey to a more satisfying life in *Red & Purple Hiking Boots: An Older Woman's Trek to "It's Never Too Late."* As a member of the Baby Boomer generation, Donna says:

> In the early years of my marriage, I assumed my role as wife was to mold myself toward the desires of my husband. If Don lived a narrow life, I was to live a narrow life. I assumed it was selfish of me to want to spend money on myself or take time away to replenish. I assumed good wives and good professionals refrained from causing conflict.

Donna began to struggle with her unquestioned assumptions in her early 50s, when she felt a deep-seated and persistent urge to visit her son in Nicaragua, where he was serving in the Peace Corps. Donna's husband did not want her to travel to a third world country alone, and he declined to go with her. Donna's boss insisted that she was needed at work, to maintain the hectic pace that was part of her daily job.

Donna feared that something bad would happen if she boarded a plane to Nicaragua against the will of these men in her life. But she did board that plane in spite of her fears.

For Donna, this one action was the beginning of an entirely new life, which involved a career change to life coach and 20-plus years of ensuing adventure travel. As I write, Donna is well into her 70s, a widow who still works with coaching clients, travels internationally, and hikes mountains.

Donna claims that much of the distress we experience regarding our roles in life comes from unquestioned assumptions. For example, we assume we must take on more roles than we can realistically manage—because someone asked us to chair a committee, run a bake sale, or serve on a task force.

We also adopt definitions of our various roles based on forces outside of ourselves, including our parents, bosses, and cultural norms. We adopt these role definitions unconsciously, not realizing that we have the right to examine the assumptions behind them. Among the nastiest of these assumptions is the one that insists that it's selfish of a woman to put her own needs on equal footing with those of others.

If your own relationship is out of balance, with his needs consistently taking precedence over yours, it's time to question your assumptions. It's at least possible that you've been unknowingly complicit in putting his needs first. It's possible that he exerts control in the marriage, in part, because you've assumed a dependent role. It's also possible that he doesn't take your dreams seriously because you don't.

In suggesting that you examine your assumptions, I'm not attributing blame, and I'm not suggesting that your problems might be entirely your fault. Marriage is a dance, and both people bring unspoken assumptions to it. It just makes sense to clarify your own assumptions before you examine your partner's.

Assumptions naturally lead to expectations. It's the expectations, whether spoken or not, that often result in feelings of weight and oppression. For example, if your partner expects you to work full-time and care for the house, you might well feel oppressed as well as resentful when you are cleaning the kitchen at 11 p.m. while your partner is watching television in the next room.

Maria divorced because her expectations and those of her partner seemed so out of alignment that they couldn't be reconciled. When the two married, Maria had been in a leadership position in her family's business. The business was a passion and priority for Maria, and she relished the challenge and travel that came with it. During her courtship with Glenn, Maria worked long hours and seldom cooked or showed interest in domestic activities. They ate out often and enjoyed what time Maria's entrepreneurial responsibilities allowed.

Once the two got married, Glenn's attitude toward Maria changed dramatically. Glenn grumbled when Maria worked late hours and complained when she had to travel. When Maria came home at 7 p.m. because of late meetings, she would find Glenn had made no effort to cook or even order in for dinner.

For reasons unfathomable to Maria, Glenn's expectations for her as his wife were not the same as his expectations for her as a dating partner. She hadn't misrepresented herself, but she now felt criticized and pressured to be someone else. The pressure permeated the household, and Maria eventually realized she didn't even like herself when she was with Glenn.

Maria wanted to save the marriage, but even counseling didn't work. Once the couple divorced, Maria began to feel like herself again. The expectations she felt in her relationship with Glenn had been toxic. She felt these expectations had been imposed upon her against her will.

When two people openly and respectfully negotiate roles and expectations, relationships can flourish. For example, Dana and Drew have a marriage that may seem old fashioned, and even undesirable, to some. Drew leads an entrepreneurial software company and earnestly desires to be the next Bill Gates. He not only works long hours; he also frequently takes clients out for dinner or drinks.

Dana has a 9-5 job as an administrative assistant. She is excellent at her job and happy to leave work at the end of the day to manage the couple's home and their children's schedules. When appropriate, Dana attends business dinners and entertains potential clients with Drew.

The relationship works because Dana and Drew have negotiated and agreed upon these roles. While it might look like Drew's needs take precedence over Dana's, that isn't how the two see it. The dance works for them. Drew appreciates Dana's role in his success and in the family, and he expresses that appreciation often.

For her part, Dana pursues a passion in yoga by teaching and attending advanced training. She also enjoys activities with many friends and organizations. In the context of this marriage, Dana continues to grow personally.

CREATING YOUR PATH FORWARD

Only you can decide what roles and relationships are healthy for you. The first step is to figure out where you want to go and accept responsibility for getting there. A well-known exchange between Alice in Wonderland and the Cheshire Cat illustrates the futility of failing to take responsibility for your own direction.

"Would you tell me, please, which way I ought to go from here?" asked Alice.

"That depends a good deal on where you want to get to," said the Cat.

"I don't much care where–" said Alice.

"Then it doesn't matter which way you go," said the Cat.

"–so long as I get SOMEWHERE," Alice added as an explanation.

"Oh, you're sure to do that," said the Cat, "if you only walk long enough."

In my workshops on goal setting, I highlight six areas of focus for a well-balanced life. Obviously, you can't tackle all six areas at the same time, but you can set goals for each. This will lead you in the right direction. If the broad task seems daunting, remember that achieving the life you want is not a sprint; it's a journey you take a single step at a time. Setting goals in each focus area serves as a roadmap to get you there.

1. Health and Wellness
    This focus area is all about the body and your physical health. Your goals might involve eating right, exercising, getting enough sleep, and keeping your body functioning at its highest level.

2. Mental, Emotional, and Spiritual
    This focus area includes all things of the mind and spirit, including education, continuous learning, and your relationship with your Higher Power. As you think about your goals involving the mind and spirit, remember the adage, "Garbage in equals garbage out." Spend your mental energy on positive things.

3. Social
    This focus area includes friends, politics, community, and travel. As you set social goals, remember that the

people you spend your time with will either help you grow or drag you down. Spend most of your time with people who share your values and aspirations. Weed out any stagnant or toxic relationships.

4. Family Relationships
    This area includes your house and home, as well as your familial relationships. Formulating goals for this part of your life will help you make sure family events get scheduled on the calendar rather than squeezed out. Formulating goals will help you complete the projects that make your home a comfortable and inviting place.

5. Business and Career
    When you set goals in this area, you create a shift from holding down a job to controlling your career. Begin by asking yourself: If all jobs paid the same and needed the same education, where would you go when you got up in the morning? If you are not going there, why not? What do you need to do to get there? Then formulate goals to get you to that job one step at a time.

6. Finances
    This focus area includes your present and future finances, your insurance needs, your philanthropic desires, and more. It includes everything and anything that has to do with controlling your finances; enjoying what your income can do; and planning for financial independence.

Given that these six focus areas encompass the all-important areas in our lives, it's appropriate to formulate goals for each. The job isn't complete until you write the goals down and state them in an affirmative way. For example, for a health goal, you might write, "I will eat at least one serving of green, leafy vegetables a day." For a career goal, you might write, "I will complete certification as a professional coach."

Once you have formulated and written goals in all six focus areas, you have an image and a roadmap of the life you desire. With your roadmap before you, decide which area is most pressing and make that area your first priority. For example, if excessive debt is creating a barrier to other goals, tackle that debt first. If your marriage or another relationship is draining all your energy, decide what you can realistically do about that relationship.

Your goals are about you, so start in the place that makes the most sense for you. Wherever you start, be sure to formulate a mixture of bigger goals and smaller ones, breaking big goals into manageable steps. We all need small successes to keep feeling positive and motivated.

For example, you might be itching to remodel your entire living room. Perhaps the couch is old, the carpet matted, and the paint dingy. Make a plan to tackle these things as you can afford them. In the meantime, buy some new throw pillows to brighten up the room and your spirits.

CREATING VACUUMS

Once you know where you want to go, you can begin to evaluate which parts of your life are moving in the right direction and which are holding you back. Then you can take appropriate action.

Can it really be that simple? Aren't some complicated problems in life insurmountable? Not really.

Two laws of nature can guide us in any unsatisfactory relationship, job, or other situation. They are:

1. Nature hates a vacuum.
2. Two things cannot exist in the same space at the same time.

When most women hear the word vacuuming, they think of their Hoover or Dyson. Vacuuming brings up visions of removing unwanted stuff off their floors and carpets. But vacuuming also means emptying a space of everything. A natural law says, "Nature hates a vacuum." This simply means that if you remove something from a space, nature will fill that space with something else. For instance, think of pouring water out of a glass. As the water flows out, air flows in.

A related natural law says, "Two things cannot exist in the same space at the same time." For example, a glass can't be filled with water and air at the same time.

Both of these laws are important in our daily living. Too many of us have filled our lives with things that are not good or valuable. We have closets full of ill-fitting, outdated clothes. We have uncomfortable home furnishings. Our living spaces are cluttered and disorganized. We have bad financial situations, bad debts. We are in unhappy or abusive relationships. We work in jobs that are unsuitable for us or bring us no satisfaction.

So, if two things can't fit in the same place at the same time, how can we bring in better clothes, better home furnishings? A better job? Happy and loving relationships?

We can't make room for the good until we have vacuumed out the bad. When the space is cleared to make room for something better, nature will fill the void. We need to review everything in our lives so that we can ask ourselves, "Does this person, place, thing, outfit, career, or situation fit the design I have for my life?"

Shakespeare said, "All the world's a stage and each must play a part." If you were writing the script for the story of your life, could you say you have assembled the right characters, scenery, and costumes to make it a smashing success? If not, create vacuums.

Most of us have complicated lives that function like a junk drawer. Too much stuff and no way to find out what we really want and need. It's time to start vacuuming. Of course, it certainly may be easier to vacuum out a worn pair of shoes or an old sweater—much easier than vacuuming out relationships and friendships that aren't working. Yet this is essential to our health. In one of my favorite quotes, Steve Maraboli reminds us, "Let go of the people who dull your shine, poison your spirit and bring you drama. Cancel your subscription to their issue."

So, ask yourself if the people who fill up your space actually bring you joy, make you a better you, support your efforts, cheer you on, and allow you to be who you really want to be. If not, get out your Hoover and vacuum.

Many women are especially reluctant to vacuum out bad relationships because they are so afraid they will be alone. Let's begin by accepting the fact that we will likely end up alone at some point. Remember the statistics for divorce and widowhood?

Women still live longer than men. So, if you are still hanging onto a disappointing, unhappy relationship, just so at the end someone will be there, he probably won't be. And you will have managed to trade years of potential happiness for years of certain misery.

If you are worried about being alone, remember that there is a huge difference between being alone and being lonely. In today's world, with women being wives, life partners, moms and daughters, members of the workforce, homemakers, sisters, caretakers, PTA members, and more, who doesn't at some point wish she could be alone?

What none of us want to be is lonely, and we don't need to be. There are so many outlets for not being lonely that if you participate in a few of them, you might actually want to be alone. Here is a partial list of options: social media and social dating sites; singles groups and single parent programs; networking organizations; educational outlets; life planning classes; community organizations; focus groups; physical fitness programs; church groups; and travel groups.

In addition to fearing loneliness, many of us succumb to a fear of failure that keeps us from changing roles or taking responsibility for our careers. We often don't create the necessary vacuums in our work lives. We are so afraid of what will happen if we don't succeed. But think about this. What's the worst that could happen? Could you end up penniless, under a bridge, with no home, no friends, no family, and no food? Well, maybe. But what are the chances? Could the worst really happen?

If the chances are remote that the worst will happen—even if the failure you will have to deal with is something less catastrophic than living under a bridge—in that case, you simply need a Plan B.

You need an alternative just in case things don't necessarily go the way you want in Plan A. Don't let fear of failure keep you hanging on to the wrong job, and don't let fear of being alone keep you hanging onto the wrong relationship. Don't let fears stop you from having the life you want. You don't want to get to the end of the journey saying, "I wish I had" instead of "I have what I wished for."

Knowing What You Know ... and Don't Know

What would it take besides desire and determination to get you where you want to be? As you put together your roadmap for your future, you might find you need help. It's okay to need help. None of us has the expertise or skill to do it all on our own. When we try to do it all alone, we create setbacks when we could be creating progress.

For example, when I finally purchased that first home many years ago, one bathroom had metallic black, silver, and orange wallpaper. I decided I had to replace that wallpaper immediately. Money was tight, so the only way I was going to be able to afford to do this was to do it myself. I rationalized that I was an intelligent, well-educated person, so I should be able to do anything.

After three days of stripping, measuring, cutting, and hanging, I discovered I clearly had no talent for wallpapering. In the end, I did what I should have done in the first place. I called a professional who charged me twice the price she normally would have because she had to undo the damage I had done before she could do it right. That experience taught me that the cheapest way is not necessarily the best way. Talent, expertise, and knowledge are invaluable tools worth paying for.

A Little Push

Now let's assume you believe you have everything you need to reach your goals, but you are still not able to take that first step to get you there. Sometimes we just need a little push to get where we are going.

A few years ago, my great-niece and I went to a resort for the weekend. We had many activities, but she was most excited about zip lining. Although I have a fear of falling, I also recognized that this would be a fun life experience. So I agreed to join in.

When we got to the zip lining launch area, my niece got harnessed up, stepped off the landing, and down into the air she went, laughing and yelling all the way. It was fun to watch her have fun—until it was my turn.

I went to the launch area and stepped into my harness. The attendant said, "Okay, Ma'am, step off." In an instant, my logical mind told me that no intelligent human being would just step off into endless space. My pounding heart told me that I should be fearful. And I was.

But this was a life experience I did not want to miss. I didn't want to disappoint my niece or myself. I had to overcome my fear.

I told the attendant that I needed her help. I needed a push. I told her that I was going to close my eyes, and when I did, she was to push me. I asked her to take control out of my hands for the moment. I asked her to make me move forward. So she did. I went sailing out into the air, opened my eyes, and had a great experience. All it took was a little push.

We all sometimes need a push in the right direction. Sometimes we need a person behind us moving us along—a coach, so to speak. Besides the obvious coaches, such as sports coaches, today there are people trained to coach us in every area of our lives. You can hire a career coach, fitness coach, or sales coach. I found that our business moved to the next level when we hired a business coach. One of my associates uses a coach to help her with her client presentations.

Sometimes the people who can give us the push we need are called consultants rather than coaches, people you can consult to get good input on how to reach your goals. You might benefit from a financial consultant, marketing consultant, investment consultant, or makeup consultant.

As you formulate your goals, factor in the help you need to accomplish those goals. If you don't have all the skills you need (and most people do not), gather a group of talented people who can complement your talents. Build a team of people who can give you that much needed push.

The best people for your team will be those who have a stake in you—people who will also benefit if you are successful. For instance, in my business, we count on certain people to provide us with products and services for our business. The more successful we are, the more successful they are. We have a synergistic reason to work together.

LESSONS FROM THE BIRDS

Over the years, I've realized that I can learn so much from the world around me. It is important that we never shut ourselves off from the people and things that enter our lives. For example, some years ago, I hung a wreath, made of vines, ribbons, and baby's breath, above the fireplace in my outdoor space. Within a month, I saw robins picking away at the wreath, taking pieces of the vine and ribbon and flying off to add it to nests they were building elsewhere.

One evening, I noticed that an industrious robin had chosen to use the wreath as the very foundation of his nest. He began by packing mud between the fireplace wall and the wreath. To discourage this building project, I removed the wreath, removed his structure, and re-hung the wreath. By the end of the next day, this determined robin had rebuilt the nest. Taking it down again, I came home the next evening to see he had built it again; and that his female partner had moved in.

I decided that such determination should be rewarded, and I left them alone. Within a few weeks, eggs appeared; and within a couple of months, baby birds were born, fed and taught to fly. Finally, the entire family left the nest. It was a nice experience to watch.

Although I removed the old nest when the original family moved out, new robin families came for the next five springs, built their nests, raised their children, and moved on. The robin families all seemed secure in my space and willing to share the space with my family. When we came outside to sit, watch TV, cook, or take in the evening air, the robin families did not fly away. They watched our activities just as we watched theirs. On occasion, after the babies were born, the mothers sometimes squawked if we got too close, just to remind us that we were sharing their space, too, after all.

Last year, something new happened. After the robin family moved away, I forgot to take down the nest. I had been traveling a lot, and upon returning from an extended trip, I was surprised to see that a male and female dove had taken up residence in the old robin's nest. Not only had they made it their home, but the doves had also added more mud, twigs, and leaves. The nest was now big enough for the two doves to sit in it side by side on two eggs.

For weeks, mama and papa dove took over my deck, flew in and out, perched on the furniture, and even sat on an outside ceiling fan, while it went round and round as the air blew past it. They were having a great time and really making themselves at home. When the babies hatched, the parents littered the area with seed pits and other food sources. Unlike the robins, they were very unwilling to share the space. They squawked anytime I came out the door and frantically flew from side to side in the space anytime someone approached.

By the time the doves moved out, the wreath that had been the foundation of all the nests and the source of building materials for so many robins had totally deteriorated; and so I took down the wreath with its nest attached and threw it away. It felt like the end of an era. But in the process of clearing out the wreath and cleaning up the space, I found myself meditating on some life lessons I had learned from this odyssey.

All of these birds were just doing what comes naturally. They were following their instincts.

They are determined to accomplish their goals, which include work, family, creativity, and song. They let nothing stand in the way of their progress. Birds are the perfect example of simplicity, joy, and abundance all rolled into one of God's small creatures.

Birds use natural elements to create a home and raise a family. The doves recycled an existing structure to adapt it to their needs.

The priority for these birds is their family; and the parents work together to create a healthy, safe, and nurturing environment. They protect their nest from outside influences. They raise their children to become independent creatures, teaching them to fly, search for food, and leave the nest.

My experience with the birds reminds me of some basic rules for living well. As you create the path for your future, remember these lessons:

1. Learn to live without stress

2. Enjoy life's simple pleasures

3. Plan, live, create

4. Work your plan, whatever you want that plan to be

5. Make the choice to be whom and what you want to be

6. Accomplish your goals

7. Let nothing stop you from living the life you choose

CHAPTER 4

PLANNING FOR
THE FUTURE

A goal without a plan is just a wish.

~ Antoine de Saint-Exupery

CHAPTER 4

PLANNING FOR THE FUTURE

I LIKED THE COMEDIAN George Carlin—not the Comedy Central, four-letter word version of George Carlin—but the philosophical, public television one.

The first time I heard Carlin's commentary on "stuff," I was struck by how insightful, as well as how funny, it was. For so many of us, life is all about our stuff.

According to Carlin, stuff is the reason we get up in the morning, go to work, earn money, and worry about money. It all has to do with stuff.

We need to buy stuff and pay for stuff. We need a place to put our stuff. A house is just a pile of stuff with a cover over it. When we get even more stuff, we need to buy a bigger house to hold it all.

We need a car to carry our stuff when we leave home. When we travel any distance, we pack our most important stuff and take it with us so we don't have to buy all new stuff when we get where we are going.

Carlin's commentary goes on and on. Although Carlin died in 2008, you can still see his routine on YouTube. It is all about "stuff."

It makes me wonder: How many important decisions have you and I made based on the kind of stuff we want? Perhaps you picked a career path or pursued a particular educational path, depending on the kind of stuff you wanted in life.

For example, if you wanted a small house with a swing set in the back yard, you may have chosen to marry a man who could provide just that. If you wanted a big office with a big desk to hold lots of stuff, you may have decided to go into business for yourself. In any case, stuff, or the accumulation of stuff, has a significant impact on your life and mine.

Over the years, our choices surrounding stuff have become incredibly vast. When I was a child, we bought groceries from the corner store. We had one or two brands to choose from. Do you remember Sealtest milk, Campbell's® soup, and Town Talk bread? With limited choices, you got in and out of the grocery store in 10 minutes. Today, when I go to my local megastore, Giant Eagle, I need to allow an hour just to find my way through the maze of choices.

Of course, you can pretty much buy any stuff you want without even going to a store. Just go online. My favorite new dot.com is Shoes.com. This site has thousands of pairs of shoes from which to choose. You can sort by size, color, heel height, and material. It all comes with free shipping and free returns. I will never go to a shoe store again.

As our choices regarding stuff have expanded, our stuff has gotten more complicated. If I don't like the many stations available on my televisions, I can choose premium stations, buy a movie, or download from Netflix—if I can work my sophisticated equipment. Sometimes it seems as if shopping or watching a screen has become so overwhelming that it is a challenge to just get started.

Having so much stuff and so many options is expensive. The phenomenon of women moving out of the home and into careers is connected, at least in part, to needing income for all the new, expensive stuff. With this relatively new reality, we need to hire other people to take care of our stuff, such as housework, lawn care, and laundry. We hire people to take care of our other living things, such as our children and our pets.

Your prosperity, the prosperity of businesses in your community, and the prosperity of our country depends on us wanting, needing, buying, selling, improving, and replacing our stuff. Even many Amish, who live simple lives, depend on creating and selling furniture (which is stuff), which they need the rest of us to buy.

STUFF IS THE PROBLEM—AND
BELIEF IN ABUNDANCE IS THE ANSWER

If the root of our problems is our preoccupation with acquiring and caring for stuff, am I suggesting we stop wanting and needing stuff? That we forgo all convenience, comfort, and choice? Not at all. The answer is to shift our perspective from a poverty to an abundance mentality.

We were put on this earth to live well, and to live abundantly. Lucille Ball once said, "I have lived meagerly and I have lived well. Living well is so much better."

But living well doesn't necessarily mean acquiring a mountain of stuff. Living well means living with peace of mind. Living abundantly means living free of money worries. It means owning your stuff rather than your stuff owning you.

An abundance mentality helps you to use your energies wisely, be in control of your emotions, and use money as a means of exchange for improving your life and the lives of those around you.

The path to an abundance mentality starts with noticing how you think about money. For example, are you aware of the attitudes about money your parents and others passed on to you? If you didn't absorb the following views as an impressionable child, you've heard them repeated often enough since:

- Money doesn't grow on trees

- Money is the root of all evil

- Blessed are the poor

These sayings represent a poverty mentality, the opposite of abundance. If you were raised to believe that only evil people are successful or wealthy, or that only the poor are humble, guilt at even the thought of being successful can crush your entrepreneurial spirit. You'll need to address this negative root belief before you can live an abundant life.

One summer, I had the chance to spend time with a voodoo queen in New Orleans and then a working witch in Salem. I was amazed to discover that I had very wrong ideas regarding what these practitioners did and what their religious beliefs entail. Both were adamant that their work emanates from the good in the world. They reject evil.

At the same time, these practitioners believe in the law of attraction, the law described in the book and movie, *The Secret*. You'll find this same law in the teachings of Jack Canfield and Tony Robbins. The law is straightforward: What you focus on is what will be attracted to your life.

In other words, if you focus on positives, you will attract positives to your life; if you focus on negatives, you will attract negatives. Our thoughts are energy that attract "like" energy. The spells the voodoo queen and working witch perform are their ways of going out to the universe and asking for (attracting) what they want.

While there is a resurgence of talk about the law of attraction, it's not new. For example, Native Americans dressed in animal skins before going out to hunt. This wasn't an attempt to camouflage themselves, but to ask the universe to attract the animals. Native Americans dressed, thought, and acted like the animals they wanted to attract.

If you want prosperity, you have to focus on it in positive ways. If you treat money shabbily, fail to respect it, or think of it negatively, you will not be able to attract it to you. The first step to abundance is to evaluate your overall relationship with money. What do you want that relationship to be? How will you bring that relationship to fruition?

Obviously, it takes time to build a positive relationship with money and attract the prosperity you need to live the life you want. You can begin by sowing seeds and reaping the results. You sow seeds in everything you do—in how you choose to view yourself, view others, and "show up" in situations. It's time to sew those seeds intentionally to attract the results you want.

One day, I was at Starbucks waiting to meet a friend for coffee. I noticed that two young men, one with dirty shoes and one with a soiled tie, were talking to a prospective client about how they could help him put a financial plan together to save for retirement. Of course, I had to tune in.

The prospect wanted to know what this plan would cost him. "Nothing," they said. "We will do it for free."

What is wrong with this picture? What were these young men sowing? With their non-professional appearances, they were sowing low self-images and low credibility. Would you (or should you) trust your retirement planning to people who can't manage to polish their shoes or wear clean ties?

What's more, services that come free have no perceived value. Giving your services away gives the impression that those services, and you as a professional, have limited worth.

Being your best and doing your best in every situation is a way to sow seeds, ones that will reap the best from others. Believe and act like everything you do has value and importance, and others will see you that way. Get a first-class education; have a first-class business; and associate with first-class people. See that even the routine activities of your day are special. Take a first-class approach to how you handle everything. For example, rather than buying four inexpensive outfits that will go out of style in one year, buy one classic, high-quality suit on sale.

Sow seeds of health, well-being, and a positive image. Take care of you. Exercise, eat right, get a massage, have your nails done. When you fail to take care of yourself, you reap medical problems, stress, and mental health problems. And, the best thing you can do for your family, your boss, your friends, your career, your clients, and your bank account is to take care of you. Remember the oxygen mask rule from air travel: You can't take care of others until you take care of yourself. Trying to do things the other way around can kill you.

Being the best you can be means letting others be the best they can be at what they do. Rather than trying to do everything yourself, hire people who can do certain things more efficiently than you can. You might delegate filing, typing, client services, housecleaning, yardwork, or changing the oil in your car. This will leave you more time to dedicate to your highest priorities.

Don't Let Budgeting Depress You.
It's Your Path to Freedom

Governments, corporations, and people like Bill Gates have budgets—because no matter how big or small your financial picture, a budget is an essential tool for financial health and prosperity. Think of it this way: When money is set aside for your essentials, everything left is yours to spend without guilt. If you understand and use the tool properly, a budget is a freeing thing.

It may surprise you to learn that the purpose of a budget is not to let you know how rich or poor you are. The purpose of a budget is not to constrain you to a less-than-abundant life. The purpose of a budget is to let you know how much money you need to live the life of your dreams.

If you have completed your budget and now think you can't afford the journey to your dreams, the budgeting process somehow failed you. It convinced you that you are poor. You need to do a new budget with a new approach.

Instead of starting with what you currently earn and spreading it out over the bills, start with all your goals and determine what they will cost. This process will tell you what your monthly income needs to be. Don't let your current situation dictate your dreams. Believe you can have anything if you truly desire and work for it.

There is no intrinsic value in being poor, and we need not accept being poor as a life option, let alone a necessity. Those who say that Scripture tells us, "Blessed are the poor," need to revisit the text, which actually says, "Blessed are the poor in spirit." The New Testament tells us that we are here to live life and live it abundantly. We can't do that if we are poor.

Poverty is not blessed, but ugly and dirty. It brings helplessness. It prevents us from enjoying all the good things in life. And no one was ever meant to live that way. Money by itself is not good or evil. It is a tool. It can be used to build or destroy. When used properly, money is the source of living well.

Financial independence begins with abundance or prosperity thinking. Life stories of some of the world's ultra-wealthy reveal that most were not born that wealthy, nor did they become wealthy overnight. Andrew Carnegie, Henry Ford, Lee Iacocca, Oprah, Tony Robbins, and so many more were poor, bankrupt, or nearly bankrupt before they went on to be incredibly wealthy and successful.

When these individuals were down, they didn't stay down, because they believed in the power of prosperity. They were grateful for what they had, set goals, and worked toward those goals. They were persistent and determined, going after their dreams with a passion. They planned for financial independence as if nothing else were an option.

After my husband died, I moved in with my mother in our family home. I felt safe and comfortable there, and, at the time, I thought I was not going to be able to raise my son on my own, emotionally or financially. Within a year, I began to realize that Christopher and I deserved a home of our own. Like most parents, I wanted to give him so much more than I had had. We lived with my mother at that time because I chose to do so. But I was able to make other choices.

Believing that a prosperous life was an option for my son and me, I assessed what resources I had, set goals, made a plan, moved out of state, and used my education to get a teaching job. I rented a small home, and to some extent was satisfied with how our life was going.

Every time I thought of buying a house, which is what I wanted, I realized that the income I was making as a teacher would never be enough. I reviewed my budget to see what I would need to earn to afford a house and the additional expenses it would bring. My teaching job was never going to bring in that kind of money. The answer to this problem was clear: Get a new job. And I did. The road wasn't easy, but it led to the life I wanted for Christopher and me.

Financial independence means having all the money you need to live the way you want to live, without having to depend on anyone or any job to provide it. Ask yourself this question: How much money would I need so that I had everything I needed, including sufficient income to cover all my bills, if I were to stop working tomorrow? If you were to lose your job tomorrow, or something should happen to prevent you from ever working again, how long could you maintain your current lifestyle? If the answer to this is not "forever," you are not financially independent, at least not yet.

Plan for Security, Peace of Mind, and Control of Your Life

Living abundantly does not mean the same thing as seeing how much stuff you can accumulate. It is "buying" peace of mind, having security in your old age, having time with your spouse, partner, or soulmate, children, and friends. Abundance is building a house and a home, having fun, helping in the community, making a difference in the world, having good health, and bringing life into balance.

None of us can achieve abundance without taking an active interest in our financial affairs. In many relationships, one partner handles all the money. Even if both partners' goals and desires are the same, it is never a good plan to have one person in control.

For example, Ann, the mother of two, wasn't particularly concerned when her husband suggested she become the family's sole breadwinner. As a corporate executive, she earned $200,000, more than enough for a Seattle-based family to live comfortably in 1999.

What's more, Ann's husband had just cashed in several million dollars' worth of Microsoft stock options. The couple decided that the windfall would go into savings, and the family would live off Ann's paychecks.

Soon after, a red flag appeared. Ann discovered that her husband had deposited the option proceeds into four separate bank accounts, only one of which shared her name. When questioned, her husband promised to change the single accounts to joint accounts. He never did.

A year later, the couple separated. Only then did Ann take a good look at the finances, only to learn she had very little money of her own. She didn't even have a claim on the proceeds of the stock options because her husband had received the grant from Microsoft one month before the wedding. In the divorce settlement, 80 percent of the stock options were considered her husband's individual assets rather than joint property.

The moral of this story: Never let go of your own purse strings. Be your own Chief Financial Officer (CFO). Even if your partner is more interested in finances than you are, you owe it to yourself to be actively involved. Even a business with a CFO holds an annual meeting. Your marriage needs that meeting too!

STRATEGIES FOR BEING CFO OF YOUR OWN LIFE

1. Decide to Change

   All positive change begins with a decision. If your financial situation is out of control, you are not saving money, you are always worrying about money, you are in debt, you are overspending, and/or you are on the verge of bankruptcy, you need to decide today that all this needs to change. Deciding to change and accepting that you have the power to do so is the single biggest step you can take.

   If you are struggling with your decision, ask yourself this question: Do I want to grasp the starring role in my life or be the stagehand in someone else's?

2. Create Vacuums

   You'll remember that nature hates a vacuum. If you create an empty space, nature will find something to fill the void.

   If you have filled your life with things that have no value to you—including bad debt, bad investments, unsatisfactory home furnishings, ill-fitting clothes, bad relationships, untrue friends, or a job you don't like—vacuum them. Nature will find a way to fill the void with something new, something better.

Take an honest look at the stuff and relationships in your life. What do you need and want? What do you need to let go?

3. Define Your Purpose and Set Goals
    Don't be overwhelmed by the need to define your purpose and set goals. You are a unique person with your own strengths, passions, and dreams. You deserve your dreams, even if people in your life have never encouraged you to believe this. Try writing the script for your ideal life, and refuse to allow anyone else to criticize it. Then formulate short-term and long-term goals to get you there.

4. Take Care of You
    One of the most important things for your finances, as well as for yourself, your family, your career, your boss, your community, is to take care of you.

    The biggest drain on a woman's finances is poor health. If you aren't in good health, you won't have the ability to advance in your career. In fact, poor health is a contributing factor in women become homeless. Invest in preventative care, healthy food, exercise, and healthy habits. This is an essential investment in your future.

2. Have a Stash of Cash
    Cash is king (or queen if you like). My mother used to keep her cash in a coffee can; we only need to keep ours in a savings vehicle. Cash is:

    - Financial freedom and control

    - The ability to leave a bad relationship

    - The safety net in an emergency

    - The vehicle that keeps us from draining retirement assets

- The vehicle that keeps us from cashing in funds at the bottom of the market

- The basis of any good financial plan

Keep enough cash available to cover three to six months' worth of expenses.

5.   Establish and Keep Good Credit

Perhaps at no other time in our country's history has your credit rating had a bigger impact on your life. Many employers are now getting credit ratings on their employees. A bad credit rating is viewed as a character flaw, even a chance the employee may do something illegal. In my field, a professional can actually lose licenses if he or she files for bankruptcy.

6.   Follow the 10-10-80 Rule

My mother followed and taught me the classic 10-10-80 rule to allocate my monthly income. Experts agree that this is a healthy way to live. The rule begins with giving 10 percent of what you make each month away. While this may seem crazy in this me-focused society, research shows that people who are generous to others and make a positive contribution to the world are happier.

The second 10 percent of what you make each month goes to savings or investment. In order to be healthy financially, you have to make a commitment to save—not just hope you have a little left over at the end of the month to put away. If you've heard advisors suggesting, "Pay yourself first," they were talking about savings. One of the best ways to get into the habit of paying yourself first is to have the money automatically transferred from your paycheck. If you don't touch it, you can't spend it!

Once giving and savings are satisfied, you can spend 80 percent of your income on living expenses and discretionary purchases, knowing that you are building a healthy financial picture.

7.   Save More Money by Saving Taxes

Most people cheat on their taxes, but not in the way you might imagine. Most taxpayers cheat themselves. Take the following steps to avoid this:

- Do your homework to be sure of all available credits and deductions

- Make the maximum 401k and IRA contributions

- Review your investments each year for capital losses

- Ask your advisors about tax harvesting

8.   Forecast for Future Needs and "Bucket" Your Money

In order to have the money you need when you need it, use a bucket strategy. For example, money you are planning to spend to purchase a house in the next six months belongs in a short-term bucket. Money earmarked for your retirement needs, a decade or more from now, belongs in a long-term bucket. With the bucket strategy, a bad market won't ruin your short-term plans.

Figure out what you will need and when you will need it. Then plan your investments based on time, not timing. Put money you will need during the next three years in a cash account. Put money you will need in the next four to seven years in bonds and equivalents. Put money you will need in the next seven to 10 years in managed portfolios. Put money you will not need for 10 or more years in the stock market.

9.   Watch What You Sign

In the busy pace of life, it can be tempting to trust others—whether the other is a professional attorney, tax professional, or your spouse—to guide you in financial or legal matters. Don't do it! You are liable for what you sign—so read first.

You don't need to be a pessimist to understand that others may lead you astray, either unintentionally or intentionally. You need only read the earlier chapters in this book for examples of how this can happen. And even people with the best intentions make mistakes and/or follow bad advice.

10. Keep Your Foot in the Door

Statistics tell us that 90 percent of women will spend some part of their adult lives as a single. In light of this statistic, none of us can realistically depend on a man to meet our financial needs. It makes good sense, whatever your relationship status, to develop and maintain marketable skills.

If you have the option not to work outside your home and that's the lifestyle you choose, great. Do something that gives you the option to return to the workplace should a sudden need arise. If you are in the workplace now, keep your skills current and growing. This is the only way to be CFO of your own life.

11. Buy Disability Insurance

Most women never purchase adequate disability insurance because they never recognize the importance of the income they produce. If you are not able to live worry-free on the income that is coming into your home right now, imagine what it would be like if you had to live on 60 percent or less of that income.

If you work for a major firm, you might receive 60 percent of your paycheck if you were disabled. If you work for a small firm, chances are you would receive nothing.

Numerous studies have found that women are seriously underinsured for health and disability. If you have not reviewed your health and disability insurance in the last three years, it's time to contact your insurance professional.

Other studies have found that male partners, spouses, employers, and insurance agents undervalue women's earning potential. Keep this in mind if one of them says, "Oh you will be all right." I don't want to see you living under a highway underpass.

IT'S YOUR LIFE PLAN—BUT NEEDS OF
PARENTS AND ADULT CHILDREN ARE FACTORS

Have you noticed that in a family of five brothers and one sister, the typical choice to take care of Mom and Dad as they age is the sister? It doesn't matter if the sister is a single parent with three children of her own, has a full-time job, and babysits her brother's children on the weekends when he has to work. And if the sister happens to be single with no children, there's no room for discussion. After all, she "doesn't really have anything going on in her life anyway."

In fairness, and because sometimes tradition dictates, the caregiver in some families is the eldest sibling, just by nature of the birth order. In other families, the caregiver is youngest as he or she was the last to leave home. Living out of state, or already taking care of elderly in-laws, usually takes a sibling out of the running. In the case of an only child, that child is "it" no matter how, no matter what, no matter where.

Thankfully, I know of no children who wouldn't be willing to care for their parents if the need arose. We want to say "thank you" for the sacrifices our parents have made in raising us. We also hope that when our time comes, our children will take care of us. Even so, "willing" is not always "able."

Caring for aging parents is an awesome task. It becomes even more difficult if you also happen to be putting kids through college, preparing for retirement, and trying to pursue what dreams you have for your own life. The sandwich generation has a nearly impossible task.

In the United States, we refer to people between the ages of 50 and 65 as Baby Boomers. In England, they call them Baby Gloomers. This term was coined as more and more British found themselves taking care of dependent parents while taking care of dependent children.

Gloomers and Boomers may find themselves taking care of still-healthy parents who did not retire financially secure while helping their own adult children who have lost jobs, divorced, or who, because of poor spending habits, have returned to their parents' home. To make matters more complicated, some of the parents needing care may be divorced and remarried, with step-children. Adult children may return to the homestead with kids of their own.

The difficulties multiply even more when aging parents are ill. Financial, ethical, and even legal and moral dilemmas arise. Hard decisions need to be made. Siblings may or may not agree.

In a 2009 issue of *More Magazine*, Donna Jackson Nakazawa shares a scary statistic:

> Although over 50 percent of marriages will ultimately end in divorce, 75 percent of marriages in which one spouse develops a chronic illness will end in divorce.

Wow! Who will take care of that chronically ill parent when his or her own spouse chooses to walk away?

Boomers who have prepared well for retirement, envisioning a happy and prosperous life down the road, may find their good planning and discipline undermined by the expectation that they be responsible for...well, everyone!

Here is the moral of this story: If your financial plan does not encompass the possibility of you being a sandwich parent, your plan is not yet complete. If you have not gotten a handle on how your situation will need to change if parents and kids return to depend on you, you have more work ahead.

You need to have the end-of-life discussion with your adult children. You also need to explain your retirement plans, and how your financial plans may or may not include those children. If you have not had these discussions, there is no time like the present.

In my practice, we see people prepare to retire comfortably, only to have things disintegrate the minute the kids need a new television, money for the grandchildren's education, or some real or spurious need. People pull principal from their income-producing assets to help their parents, buy cars for their adult children, or to pay the grandchildren's college loans.

It can be extremely difficult for individuals who are givers to accept the negative impact their generosity to the takers will have on their lifestyle. All financial decisions have consequences.

What can you do to prepare a future that won't be sabotaged by the needs or irresponsibility of family members?

Develop a sound plan for financial independence. Know what you can afford and what you can't afford to give. Learn to say "no" to requests for money you cannot afford. If you lend money, get a repayment agreement in writing; have loan recipients pledge assets or insurances.

Set and reset your priorities. Prepare a solid estate plan. Build contingency planning into your retirement plans. Have adequate life and long-term care insurance, and see that those who may become dependent on you do the same.

Just as a good umbrella can shelter you from the gloom of a rainy day, a good financial and estate plan can shelter you from a financial rainy day. Then you can become a Baby Boomer instead of a Baby Gloomer.

Remember the Ultimate Goal of Your Plan

Consider this quote by Samuel Johnson, "To be happy at home is the ultimate result of all ambition …" We could wisely meditate on this one sentence for a lifetime.

Engrave these words on your consciousness. Keep them as true north while you make your life plan and the financial decisions that support it. Lay the track so deeply that even when you're on your own version of automatic pilot, you'll be homeward bound.

Remember that the definition of abundance is not the accumulation of things, and the definition of success is not the amount of your net worth. The ultimate goal of all our planning and effort is to be happy at home and in mutually-supportive relationships with the ones we love.

I once read a story about a man named Donny who was diagnosed with cancer and given only a year to live. Donny made a decision to make every day special, and he knew he needed a way to remind himself of this decision every day. He didn't want to waste even a single day.

Donny filled a glass jar with 365 small, round beads. Each morning, he removed a bead and made a plan to make the next 24 hours special. Then he threw the bead away.

When I first heard this story, I thought it was sad and morbid. I thought it would be horrible to watch your days slip by as the jar became increasingly empty. Then I learned that Donny was still alive when his jar of beads was empty. In fact, Donny filled the jar again and lived another six months. Donny deliberately lived and experienced 545 special days.

Can any of us, no matter what age, say we have planned and executed 545 special days? Mostly, we squander our time, expecting there is more to come. If our life expectancy as women is roughly 80 years, how many days do we have left? How many beads are in my jar? Yours?

Thinking about the diminishing days before us is not a reason to be sad. It's a reason to make every day we have special. Each of us has the power to embrace our days or squander them. We have the power to use our time to make the world a better place or to spend it in accumulating and caring for increasingly more stuff. Ultimately, your financial plan is your life plan. Choose wisely. Choose abundance.

CHAPTER 5

STAGES OF FINANCIAL LIVES

You can always alter and adapt your plan, provided you have one.

~ Manoj Arora,
From the Rat Race to Financial Freedom

CHAPTER 5

STAGES OF FINANCIAL LIVES

WE FORM OUR ATTITUDES AND HABITS about money during our earliest years of life. We absorb our parents' attitudes about money, including the messages in their clichés. In some families, the messages are all about lack. For example, children in those families might hear the mantra, "Money doesn't grow on trees." In other families, the messages are about abundance. Children in those families might hear, "You can have whatever you want if you are willing to work for it."

We are shaped by our parents' behaviors surrounding money, too, whether we are consciously paying attention or not. Individuals who grow up in families of savers tend to think saving is normal. Those who grow up in families of over-spenders are inclined to think debt is normal. Those who grow up in families with conflicting views surrounding money may experience lasting tension and anxiety around the topic.

There's no doubt: Your growing up years have shaped your views and behaviors about money. If you haven't already done so, it's time to pay attention to those influences. From an objective perspective, are the attitudes you hold smart and healthy? Will they lead to the life you want for yourself?

I was fortunate to grow up in a home where the messages about money were productive. While my single mother didn't have much money, she knew how to stretch what she had. She was fun and creative, helping us to feel blessed, if not rich. She also taught us that a different financial picture was possible for us in the future, that we had control over what we could achieve.

When my son, Christopher, was 5 or 6 years old, he desperately wanted a specific set of Matchbox cars. The set cost around $10, which was real money for me at that time. I told Christopher that if he could raise $2, I would donate the rest of the money to purchase the set.

Christopher did chores for me and his grandmother, steadily growing his savings a nickel or a quarter at a time. Then, one day, Christopher's grandfather on my deceased husband's side came to visit. When his grandfather learned about Christopher's earning project, he offered to give Christopher the $2. At the age of 5 or 6, Christopher already knew that this wasn't how money was supposed to work. He declined the offer, proceeded to earn the money, and got his Matchbox cars. Christopher already knew that money for things you want has to be earned.

This was perhaps Christopher's first life event in which he had to evaluate his beliefs about money and make a financial decision. In the scope of life, it wasn't a big event, and yet the sense of pride and satisfaction Christopher got by earning his portion to buy the cars was a big deal.

Each of us faces many events in which we have to make financial decisions and face the consequences. This chapter considers financial issues and decisions that arrive predictably throughout stages of a woman's life, including decisions about education, a first job, home ownership, and more. As a financial planner, I routinely work with women in each of these stages. My goal is to share the best practices I've learned along the way.

Education

Among the most pressure-packed issues in the life of an emerging adult woman is choosing a career and the educational path to get there. Her friends or boyfriend may have already made their choices; her parents may have strong views about their alma mater; she may or may not want to be far from home; and more.

The young woman may have an idea of what she wants to do for her career, but not know much about the jobs and salaries in that field. Many high school students simply pick a college that appeals to them and trust that a job will arrive like the pot of gold at the end of the rainbow. They buy into the idea that the college years are for fun, and life only gets serious at graduation. This is a deeply-rooted and potentially-disastrous myth in our culture.

Unless you get a free ride, college is a significant financial decision, one that can easily burden you with unnecessary debt for many years. In fact, student debt is a lifestyle choice you have to live with.

In my practice, I see too many young people who have made foolish financial decisions surrounding college. For example, Valerie spent $42,000 a year to attend a private college to become a teacher. A degree from a state school would have qualified Valerie for that job for half that amount.

Had she chosen to go to a state school, Valerie could have saved $84,000. Because she didn't think through the financial commitment she was making, Valerie had to build her adult life on a foundation of debt. This affected her ability to purchase the home she wanted, and she entered marriage and parenthood financially restricted. It didn't have to be that way.

Another client, Natalie, went to college to become a music teacher. Natalie was passionate about music, and she dreamed of making a difference in her students' lives. Unfortunately, most schools are shrinking their music departments, not hiring new teachers. Had Natalie done some research before investing money and four years of her life developing skills that don't fit the marketplace, she'd be in a far better financial position today.

If you are entering college or preparing for a career, above all, be realistic. The financial burdens you assume to pay for an education don't go away until you pay off the loan. Don't make a commitment to pay for more education than you need.

As you consider careers, think carefully about the kind of lifestyle you want. Then do your research. First, find out if the job you want is in demand in the marketplace. Then find out what that job pays—if it will support the lifestyle of your choice. This information is readily available. Use it!

Parents, remember that the educational choices your children make can and will affect *your* financial future. If you co-sign for a loan, you may have too much debt to afford your retirement home. Or even qualify for the best interest rate on your next car.

If your child dies, becomes disabled, loses a job, or behaves irresponsibly, you are on the hook. If your child becomes over-whelmed with debt, he or she may move in or stay in your home, seriously changing your retirement plans.

First Job

If you make good educational decisions, your job opportunities should match the lifestyle you choose. Before you start job hunting, however, create a budget to see what you'll need. Then look for the job. You need the budget information to know if an opportunity makes sense for you. If the job doesn't support the lifestyle you want, you have some choices. You can look for another job, make less expensive lifestyle choices, or choose a lifestyle of debt.

As you consider any job opportunity, ask detailed questions about the benefits. Don't make any assumptions about benefits. Learn the company's benefits involving life insurance, disability, retirement contributions, and medical insurance. Don't be presumptuous about being young and healthy. Everyone is vulnerable to life's unpredictability.

I learned recently about Karl, a man who had a good job at a bank. Karl's wife was pregnant and the couple was looking forward to their first child. When Karl was offered a job at another bank with an increase in salary, he jumped at the chance. Only later did Karl learn that his new medical insurance wouldn't kick in until he had been on the job for six months. He also learned that the new job provided less life insurance and decreased medical coverage in comparison with the job he left. A big part of Karl's pay raise went to secure the benefits he lost.

Individuals beginning their first job as adults naturally assume a long life ahead. They naturally want to enjoy what they earn. If those individuals are smart, however, they develop a five-year plan before they start spending. The plan specifies how they will pay off any debt and how they will finance their goals.

At this stage of life, it's a good idea to begin practicing the 10-10-80 rule if you haven't already done so. Giving 10 percent away sets a foundation for experiencing satisfaction and the joy of giving. Saving 10 percent allows you to develop an emergency fund, which you should do before you purchase that big screen television you want. You can spend the 80 percent as needed without worry or guilt.

Don't wait until you are older to participate in stock options or 401K plans at your job. The earlier you save for retirement, the more quickly your nest egg will multiply. The compound interest that comes with saving young will give you an edge. It's impossible to achieve that particular edge when you begin saving later.

YOUNG AND SINGLE

As you navigate your way through your young adult years, you will be faced with a number of lifestyle choices. For starters, will you buy a home or rent? Either choice has its tradeoffs. When you choose to rent, you transfer the risk and responsibility of your residence to someone else. If a major repair expense comes unexpectedly, you won't have to pay for it.

On the other hand, if you buy a house, you build equity in that home with your mortgage payments. At the same time, you assume responsibility for routine maintenance and assume the risk of ownership. If you choose to purchase a house, make sure to establish an emergency fund to pay for unexpected expenses, such as a broken furnace or a failing roof.

The decision to buy or lease a car follows the same logic as the decision to buy or rent a home. In any case, be sure to have property and casualty insurance.

At every stage in life, you need a budget to predict your income needs. You also need a strategy to protect the income you depend on. If you have employee benefits that provide disability insurance, medical insurance, and life insurance, use those benefits. If you don't have the benefits, don't skimp on the insurance. It makes no sense to insure your house but not the income that pays the mortgage.

ENGAGED TO BE MARRIED

If you are considering marrying, insist on important discussions that could affect your finances. I suggest that every engaged couple have a pre-nuptial conversation, even if they don't complete a legal agreement. It's not disloyal to have this conversation; it's essential for a good foundation as much as it is for your protection. Each individual should write out the following:

- A list of assets

- A list of debt

- An explanation of how they view money

- Their expectations regarding who in the relationship should handle what chores and decisions

Have honest discussions, even if they are difficult. Resolve your issues before you marry. Come to an agreement on how you will title your various assets, such as the house and car—because with the title comes ownership. There are no right and wrong answers in these discussions. What's important is that you understand each other, work together, and realize that every decision has its consequences.

In planning for your life together, give the same attention to legal documents as you do to wedding plans. Create wills, power of attorney, and documents dictating privacy issues.

YOUNG MARRIED

It may seem pessimistic or as if you are asking for trouble in establishing your financial independence at the same time you are getting married. It's not pessimistic; it's just smart. All women, even those in good marriages, are healthiest and happiest over the long haul if they have independence. Work out your own budget, identifying what you need to live should you find yourself alone. Have accounts of your own and a stash of cash. Insure your assets to protect them. A credit history of your own, a stash of cash, and insurance give you choices should your life circumstances change by choice or by chance.

Even if you are blissfully happy in your marriage and have no interest in your finances, you should join in the planning and decision-making on how you spend and save money. Think of it this way: A marriage is like a corporation in which each member of the executive team brings talents to the organization. Annually, the executive team comes together for the "state of the union." This is as important in a marriage as it is in a corporation.

Even young married couples should have wills and an estate plan. You can adjust these as your life circumstances change, but don't live without them.

PARENTHOOD

With parenthood comes great joys and definite financial challenges. The balance between nurturing your children and providing for them is tricky.

Some moms have the choice to stay out of the workforce and wonder whether they should. Either choice is fine, as long as you realize that each has its consequences. Consider your finances, your priorities, your own sense of balance, and more.

If you take time off from your career, make sure you understand your sources of income and the options available to you should your husband unexpectedly no longer be in the picture. Protect your sources of income with insurance. Keep your resume up to date and participate in activities that demonstrate transferable skills. Continue to add to your retirement plans, understanding that you won't be contributing to Social Security during the years you are out of the workforce.

As your children grow, you'll make countless decisions that involve your financial picture. The best advice is simple: Don't do things you can't afford. For example, if you can't afford the private school, don't go there. If you can't afford for your kids to participate in multiple sports, insist that they choose the one they like best. If a neighbor child has a pony and you can't afford one, don't entertain the idea.

Teach your children to have realistic expectations based on the family situation, even as they know that they have the ability to work hard to achieve their dreams. At the same time, be careful about the pressure you put on your kids. It's wise to put away money for college rather than gamble on your kids getting scholarships. The expectation to earn a scholarship can be a tough burden for a young person.

It's natural for parents to want to take care of their kids, even to leave them an inheritance. As you plan, be realistic about the fact that you will likely need some kind of help when you age. Think about where you will be when your kids are parents themselves. Make sure you'll be able to pay for the things you will need.

I had a client whose 70-something parents inherited money. The parents wanted to start giving the money to their adult kids right away. The kids politely declined, realizing that their own lives were full of the responsibilities of raising their families. They asked their parents to buy long-term health insurance to ensure the parents would have the care they needed for the rest of their lives.

It bears repeating that every major decision, like choosing to step out of the workforce, or giving large gifts to children, has consequences. It's a good idea to talk to a professional about the consequences of these types of decisions. Then you can make the decisions that support your values and desired lifestyle.

DIVORCED

No one marries with the expectation of divorcing. On the other hand, no one buys a house expecting it to catch fire or buys a car with the expectation of a collision. At the same time, nearly everyone insures the house and the car against financial disaster, without thinking twice. Yet, when I suggest a woman prepares financially for divorce or widowhood, she is typically surprised. She may think it's a pessimistic way to look at life or a way to send a message that she doesn't really love her husband. In reality, preparing for such possibilities is simply realistic.

Some statistics indicate that 50 percent of couples will divorce. According to the U.S. Census Bureau, nearly 700,000 women lose their husbands each year. These women will be widows for an average of 14 years. Failure to have a Plan B is akin to putting your head in the sand. Hopefully, you won't ever face divorce or your spouse's death, but realism demands you prepare for either.

In either eventuality, people get through the crisis better if they have certain things in order. These things include easy access to financial statements and legal documents, a budget detailing income and housing needs, and a separate checking account.

If you see a divorce coming, meet with a divorce financial advisor before you meet with a divorce attorney. The professionals can help you keep the emotion out of the decisions so that you can make good choices. Every decision has its consequences, and you need to think both long-term and objectively. For example, women in a divorce most often want the house and the kids. They get the equity in the house, and no money. There's nothing wrong with this decision, as long as the woman has a way to pay her living expenses.

If you anticipate a divorce, you may do well to meet with a career counselor and/or a therapist, depending on your situation. Once again, the professionals can help you separate your emotions from your decisions.

After a divorce, revisit your lifestyle goals, budget, and career options. Develop your own financial plan for the next five years. Protect your assets and income. For example, if you receive alimony and/or child support, also own life insurance on your ex-husband, even if he pays the bill. When you own the insurance, you will know if the premiums are being paid. If not, you can take action.

The financial realities of a divorce affect your children in many ways: emotionally, socially, and educationally. Set an optimistic and can-do example for your kids and talk to them about how to cope with the changes. Redo your estate planning and beneficiaries to reflect the new reality of your family.

Widowed

Chances are you've heard the following and good advice for new widows: Don't make any big changes or definite plans for a year. In other words, if you can't undo it, don't commit to it. While grieving doesn't stop in a year, the feelings are ever-present and especially intense during that first year. Take the time you need to grieve and get professional help. It's natural and normal to need both time and help. If you try to make plans during deep grief, you'll have difficulty separating your emotions from your decisions. You'll be vulnerable to poor decisions that may have long-lasting consequences.

Get professional help to settle the estate. Review all your assets and transfer the ownership to yourself. Maintain liquidity and flexibility, knowing that you'll be a different person five years from now. Work with a financial educator to ensure you have the knowledge you need to take charge of your financial life. With this person's help, assess all your income needs and sources. Ensure you have adequate insurance to protect your assets and income. Redo your estate planning and beneficiaries.

As a widow, you'll need to revisit your lifestyle goals, budget, and career options—but don't panic and think you have to rethink your entire life in the first few months. Give yourself the time you need to grieve. When things begin to settle, develop your own five-year financial plan.

Pre-retirement/Retirement

I tell my clients that the goal in retirement is to spend your last dollar on your last day. Unfortunately, except in unusual circumstances, none of us knows when that last day will be. Given that the average lifespan of woman is 79 years, coupled with the rising cost of healthcare, we'd be foolish not to carefully plan for retirement. In fact, the smartest way to prepare for retirement is to begin with your first job and keep retirement savings as a priority throughout your working years.

When you are facing retirement, review your lifestyle goals in light of this new phase of life. Think about where you want to live and how you will keep healthy and active. Consider an encore career to boost your finances as well as to enjoy contributing your gifts and talents.

Set lifestyle goals for the years when your body no longer functions as it does now. Think about both independence and safety. Tradeoffs come with each. Communicate your priorities and lifestyle goals to family members long before your body becomes frail.

Once you set lifestyle goals, it is time once again to review your sources of income and prepare a budget. Armed with this information, consult with a financial expert. The expert will help you identify various choices and their consequences. Given the complexity of the financial markets, tax laws, inflation, and more, good decisions depend on clear understanding of your options and their consequences.

Be sure to review all your insurance coverages and asset protection. You'll also want to review your estate plan and beneficiaries. Develop an asset transfer plan for any money left at your death.

AT ANY STAGE, IT'S OKAY TO ASK FOR HELP

In the movie *A Streetcar Named Desire*, the character, Blanche DuBois, says, "I've always depended on the kindness of strangers." Sometimes we all need to do this. We need to ask for help where we would not necessarily expect it would come from.

A friend, Celia, and I once went by train to the Hershey Spa. I love the train. It's my favorite form of transportation. There are no long security lines (no security lines at all), great big reclining seats, free Wi-Fi, nice people, and lots of room to move around. Trains have a Club Car, Sightseeing Car, and sometimes a Movie Car. Train trips are inexpensive. If you have the time, a train trip is an overall great experience.

Most of all, trains have employees who are helpful, caring, and pleasant.

Nothing proved this reality more than when Celia and I got on the train for our return trip from Hershey to Pittsburgh. As the train pulled away from the station, we realized we were on the wrong train, going in the wrong direction. This is not an unusual experience, we learned, as you do not have to give the train personnel your ticket until after the train has departed the station. People often get on the wrong train. It was, however, an unusual and unexpected experience for Celia and me.

Fear and trepidation occurred. Celia needed to be in Pittsburgh early the next morning to see her daughter participate in a very important competition, and we were headed for New York City. We had a choice to panic, and we did that briefly. Then we realized that panic would not resolve the issue. What we needed was to make a choice to ask for help.

The engineer on the train was a woman. We found her and told her our plight. We emphasized the fact that being in Pittsburgh the next day was imperative. Celia and I were busy brainstorming various ideas, ranging from getting to the next stop and renting a car to drive home to calling a car to get us to the closet airport.

As we fretted and planned, the engineer asked us to sit down and give her a moment to make a call. She reassured us that everything would be all right.

The engineer stepped away and came back in a few minutes with a smile on her face. She told us that she had called Amtrak corporate and explained our dilemma. They told her the train that we needed to be on would be passing the train we were on in just a few minutes. They had called ahead to tell that train to stop, and they gave permission for the train we were on to stop at the same time.

The engineer and a co-worker grabbed our bags and got us ready. When the train to Pittsburgh came near, they helped us off the train onto the road and waited with us as the other train neared. When it stopped, they helped us on and hurried to get back to their train and go on their way. Before they left, the two hugged us, wished us a safe trip, and expressed their hope that Celia's daughter would win her competition. The entire Amtrak train system shut down for three minutes because the engineer and a few people at the corporate level thought it was important for us to get home.

Whatever your stage in life, be responsible. When appropriate, ask the professionals. Also, ask those you know and ask those you would like to know. Like Blanche in *A Streetcar Named Desire*, know that you can always depend on the "kindness of strangers."

BIG FINANCIAL STRATEGIES FOR SMALL BUSINESSES

The goal isn't more money. The goal is living life on your terms.

~ Chris Brogan

CHAPTER 6

BIG FINANCIAL STRATEGIES
FOR
SMALL BUSINESSES

IS THE IDEA OF FINANCIAL FAILURE a nightmare of yours? Will your money run out before you run out? Do you know how much money you need to live financially independent until you die?

Some studies indicate that the greatest fear of 70 percent of women is that they will lose everything and become a bag lady. The greatest fear of men is that they will lose their jobs and then their homes.

These fears are a reason many people today are looking for a business as their primary source of income, a supplement to their current income, an alternative to the traditional job, or an opportunity to grow wealth. Many hope to accomplish this through a non-traditional business, a home-based business, a downline, or Internet-based business.

Owning a business seems so easy, doesn't it? People say, "You own your own business, so your time is your own."

The business owner answers, "Yes, I only work half a day: the first 12-18 hours.

People say, "You make your own rules!"

The business owner responds, "Sure, I get to make the rules, after I meet the rules and expectations of the government, the bank, and the client. These are the joys of business ownership."

Because I don't require much sleep, I watch television in the wee hours of the morning. The advertisers on those late-night infomercials count on the fact that those watching are up all night worrying about money. The advertisers supply the answer: real estate, Internet marketing, product sales, and cash-flow programs. Unfortunately, the old adage applies: If it sounds too good to be true, it probably is. Buyer beware.

None of this means that owning a business is a bad idea. It means you need to think, analyze, and plan carefully before you decide to take the plunge.

BEGINNING POINT FOR A SUCCESSFUL BUSINESS

Your business, like any business, will only accomplish your financial goals if it is sound financially. So what is the bottom line?

As a business owner, you need to make money—and not just some money You need to make enough to cover your expenses, pay for your lifestyle, and provide all the benefits that a traditional job would provide. These expenses all need to be met before you can make revenue to build wealth.

You need to prepare to spend money before you make money for yourself. If you don't produce enough money to pay your expenses and more, you become a nonprofit. Chances are that becoming a nonprofit is not your goal in going into business.

The average small business spends 30 to 40 percent of its income on expenses. How does that translate into practical terms? If you are accustomed to a salary or want a salary of $40,000 a year, your business needs to gross $52,000 to $56,000.

I venture to guess that your idea of owning a business includes making a six-figure salary, or a good salary plus the flexibility of being your own boss, setting your own hours, and spending more time with your family.

None of this comes automatically to a business owner. So how do you get there?

THE MAGIC FORMULA FOR BUSINESS SUCCESS

You might be reading this book because you think there must be a magic formula. There is!

For you to succeed in business, you need to do the following:

1. Get in front of more people;
2. More often; and
3. Sell them more stuff.
4. Repeat.

All successful businesses, from Disney to Martha Stewart, from your local bank to your local grocery chain, do exactly this.

The fundamental path to success in business requires action, action, action—not just sometimes, but all the time. The most important thing is not a good business idea, a great education, or a good bankroll. The most important thing in business is persistence. Successful people get up every day, get in front of people, and sell their stuff. They do this on days they feel like it and on days they don't.

Here is the reason this formula is so important: Asking someone to buy your product or use your services is the only thing in your business that you can totally control. You can't control who buys or how much they buy, but you can control the asking. Getting in front of more people more often with your sales message increases the chances that you'll sell more. This formula constitutes the most important part of your businesses financial plan.

FORMULATING YOUR BUSINESS PLAN,
MARKETING STRATEGY, AND SALES STRATEGY

The first part of the formula—get in front of more people—is your business plan. You can't know which people, however, until you have formulated your mission. Decide what you are going to do, with whom you are going to do it, and who your clients or customers will be. All successful businesses have a business plan.

Be specific and targeted about these things. It may seem counterintuitive, but you'll be more successful if you cast your net narrow rather than wide. For example, you are likely to do better with a target market of female customers just entering the job market than you are trying to appeal to every female in the universe. Having a specific target market doesn't work to exclude potential customers; it works to draw best-fit customers to you.

The more identifiers you have for your target market, the easier it is to get in front of them successfully. Answer the following questions:

1. Are the people in my target market willing and able to spend money on my product or service?

2. Can I make enough sales from these people to pay my expenses and make a profit?

3. Will it be easy enough for me to find these people or for them to find me?

4. Are these people already loyal to another provider? If so, what incentive will I give them to try my product or service?

5. Is it likely these people will act as a referral source to help me grow my business?

Once you've identified your target market, you have to be able tell them what you do clearly, concisely, and confidently. I've been to many networking events in which each woman attendee has the opportunity to stand up and give her 90-second "pitch." The women often stumble around, providing a vague answer and projecting an image of incompetence. Such presenters don't walk away with customers or referrals.

To build a foundation for success, practice saying what you do in one or two sentences. Your "pitch" should say what you do and for whom you do it. For example, "I sell upscale clothing for mature women." For another example, "My firm builds affordable websites for startups and small businesses."

You might also consider describing your ideal client. For example, "My ideal client is a woman who wants a full-service shop where she receives personal attention—a place she can go for everything from golf outfits to formals, and everything in between. She wants a shop she can rely on." For another example, "An online presence is so important to startups and small businesses, but business owners don't have time to figure it all out. Our clients thank us for taking the headaches and hassles out of the process so they can focus on other business tasks, like serving customers."

Once you can describe your business clearly, concisely, and confidently, you are ready to get in front of prospects. Consider this: If you promoted your product or service to 20 people a day, would your business be successful? Assuming the 20 people are to some degree motivated to buy your type of product or service, the answer is Yes!

The second part of this formula is your marketing plan. Once you've identified your target market, make a plan to get in front of those people—consistently. Marketing isn't a once-in-awhile activity. Consistency and persistence is the key to success.

The third part of the formula—sell them more stuff—is your sales strategy. Answer the following questions:

1. Who is going to do the selling?
2. How will I train them?
3. How will I price my product?
4. Who will be my competition?
5. What makes me different so that people will buy from me and not my competition?

So you need a business plan, a marketing plan, and a sales strategy: Get in front of more people, more often, and sell them more stuff. Name any successful business, be it Avon, General

Motors, or Microsoft, and you will find that they got in front of more people, more often, and sold them more stuff.

Of course, at General Motors, they have a CEO, a CFO, a marketing department, a vice president of sales, and a director of employee benefits. They have bosses, managers, and employees.

In your business who are all of these people? In your small business, you are likely the CEO, CFO, marketing department, sales director, and employee benefits manager.

Every day you wear many hats, and there are things you need to do until you are successful enough to hire others to do them for you. In any case, these things need to be done. No successful business overlooks these important tasks. Start now so when you are a big company, all these things will be in place.

As both the boss and the employee of your business, be sure to evaluate your own performance. At the end of each day, you, the boss, need to review the work done by you, the employee. Are you completing the most important tasks, or just the easy ones?

Ask yourself this question: If you, the boss, had another employee who did the work that you, the employee, did on any given day, would that employee still have a job? If not, you may not be living up to your responsibilities.

BIG BUSINESS FINANCIAL
STRATEGIES FOR SMALL BUSINESS OWNERS

You don't have to be a big corporation to adopt proven big business strategies. Here are appropriate strategies for any size business:

1. Focus

    Failing to specialize can ruin a business. Decide your specialty and then do that one thing well—better than your competitors do. No one has the ability to be a successful model and a successful brain surgeon at the same time.

    I once had a client who had a successful hotdog stand. Everything was going well until the owner's son returned from college. The son was full of ideas for expansion, and he convinced his father to cut back on the hotdogs. People stopped coming.

2. Decide on Your Business Structure
   Learn how the following structures work:

   - Sole proprietorship

   - Partnership

   - LLC

   - S or C corporation

   Be sure to know the advantages and disadvantages with each, including how your business structure can protect you, your personal assets, and save you taxes at the same time. If you are just starting, start out right. If you already own a business, review your structure with an accountant, attorney, or financial advisor. Don't assume you have the best structure in place. Find out.

3. Keep a Stash of Cash
   Chances are you've heard that most small businesses fail in the first five years. Typically, this happens because the owner expects to start making money right away. No matter how wonderful your product, you may not make money in the first few years.

   On my commute to and from work, I drive through a business district filled with shops. In any three-month period, a number of businesses turn over. For example, Susie's Sweater Shop becomes Joyce's Gift Shop. This doesn't mean the business was not a good idea or that the owner didn't have good skills1qa. Often it means the owner failed to have enough cash to support the business until it became profitable.

   Read the stories of Mark Victor Hansen, Mary Kay, or other successful entrepreneurs, and you will find that he or she failed many times before succeeding. Be prepared for a slow start.

4. Prepare and Follow a Budget

    All successful businesses have budgets. As CFO of your business, it's your job to create a budget. How else will you know what you need to earn, and when you earn it, how to spend it?

    Know what you have available to spend. Know what your product or service costs to produce, as well as the percentage of the sales price you get to keep. Know what bills you have to pay.

    If you don't know how to budget, use some of your cash to hire a financial consultant or accountant to help you prepare a budget. You don't need to try to be everything on your own.

    Budget for a marketing plan so you can afford this important aspect of your business plan. Figure out what it will cost to get in front of more people on an ongoing basis. You may even want to budget to hire a marketing person.

5. Keep Good Credit

    There are times when it makes sense to use someone else's money instead of your own—but you can't get that money without good credit. Good credit allows you to lease things you need, such as equipment, furniture, and computers, instead of buying them outright. Each time we have wanted to expand our business, buy supplies, or hire help, our good credit has gotten us in the door.

    Again, you are the CFO. It is your responsibility to keep good credit. Pay the bills on time. If you don't have the time to do that, hire a CFO. There are companies where you can hire a CPA, CFO or marketing person by the hour. Such individuals don't need to be your employees; you can pay for them on an as-needed basis.

6. Keep Good Financial Records

    From a tax standpoint, small businesses are on the chopping block. The IRS looks for bogus deductions and lack of quality records. Get a financial computer program and have someone teach you to use it. You can also hire an accountant or a financial advisor to help you set up a system.

    Being in business for yourself brings you a multitude of opportunities to save on taxes, but only if you know how to take advantage of them. Successful businesses accumulate more money saving taxes than they do saving money.

    You need good records for tax purposes, but there are other reasons to keep good records as well. Looking at our financials periodically tells us so much about who we are and what we are doing. It is great to look back and see how our business has grown over the last 30+ years. Knowing how far we've come inspires us to grow even more.

7. Provide Employee Benefits

    As a business owner, you are also the employee benefits department and the HR department. That means that you need to provide yourself and any possible employees with benefits.

    If you are thinking you can't afford to provide benefits, I am here to say that you cannot afford not to. Beware: One reason small businesses close is lack of benefits.

    Benefits start with a regular paycheck. If you don't get paid, how will you pay the electric bill, the staff, the postage, and the website designer?

    You need medical and other insurances, and you may qualify for a group purchase price. There are such things as "a group of one." You also need disability insurance—the most important insurance you probably don't own. If you can't work in your own business, who will? Don't forget to purchase life insurance, too. If someone depends on your income, that someone depends on you.

8. Prepare for Retirement

    As a business owner, you are eligible for retirement plans just for businesses. Saving for retirement can help you save on taxes. Your business will not make you financially independent until you are able to retire comfortably.

9. Create Vacuums

    You'll remember how creating a vacuum works. Examining the things in your life and creating healthy vacuums is an ongoing process. Review everything from your business relationships to your clients, to your work environment and ask yourself: Does this person, place, client, sales strategy, product, or thing fit into the design that I have for my business? If not, create a vacuum.

    Eighty percent of sales for any business come from 20 percent of its clients. To be successful, you need to spend 80 percent of your time with this 20 percent. Eliminate or delegate processes that put you in front of the other 80 percent instead of in front of this 20 percent. For example, we used to do quarterly reviews with all of our clients. Then we realized that any additional fees we received came from the top 20 percent. Now we do quarterly reviews with the top 20 percent and annual reviews with everyone else.

10. Get Rid of the Parade "Rainers"

    Just when you think you've found the right business opportunity, just when you are up and running, or just when you have your business on a roll and know you are where you need to be, you can expect to run into "Negative Nancys." These people want to rain on your parade, tell you what a mistake you are making, and assure you that things won't work out for you. Parade "Rainers" will tell you about someone they know—someone smarter and more qualified than you are—who wasn't able to make it in business. My suggestion: Vacuum these people from your life.

11. Sow What You Want to Reap

    If you sow corn seeds, you will not grow tomatoes. If you plant daisies, you will not get roses.

    Whatever you would like to have in your business, sow it, care for it, and watch it grow. If you want a successful business with successful clients, you need to sow the seeds for creating this success. Sometimes this means spending money on these seeds. Establish a budget for the business that includes money to sow the seeds.

    Seeds include extensive knowledge of your products, networking in the right places, having the right educational credentials or certifications, belonging to the right organizations, and presenting a professional image. Planting such seeds won't bring instant success, but the seeds will grow if you care for them.

12. Cultivate a First-Class Image

    My college roommate was fond of saying, "It only takes a nickel more to go first class." If you are creative, this is true.

    Image is everything to successful businesses because many financial decisions have little to do with money. Don't miss this point. When someone hears your name, it's important that person thinks of your success. Add to your budget those things that will provide you with the image you want out in the world in which you thrive. If you need to reduce expenses, do it somewhere else. For example, I know a woman just starting out in business who can't afford the best clothes, yet she always looks first class. She shops for clothes at resale shops in the most affluent part of her town. It's not unusual for her to purchase clothes that still have the original sales tags on.

    Believe and act like everything you do has value and importance and others will see you that way. Get a first-class education, have a first-class business, associate with first-class people, and see to it that even the routine activities of your day are special. Take a first-class approach to how you handle everything.

13. Value Your Time and Expertise

    When I was first starting out in insurance sales, the owner of the agency told me he didn't hire women because women don't value their time. He had a valid point. For my first sale as a financial advisor, I drove 30 miles in a snowstorm to make $12. I've come a long way since then, but I meet women all the time who devalue their time, give professional advice and services away, and adjust prices for people who claim not to have the money to pay full price. Valuing your time and sticking to your fees sends the message that you are a professional who is worth a prospect's investment.

14. Project a Friendly Business Message

    Recently, a few new businesses opened near our office. One afternoon, my business partner and I decided to take a walk and visit these shops.

    The first store had a name that indicated it sold decorative household items. Upon entering the store, we discovered it was a woman's accessory store. As we looked around, the woman who seemed to be the owner stayed behind the counter talking to a friend. She never greeted us. Feeling ignored, we left, with the impression that customers weren't important there.

    The next store, a flower shop, had a small gate blocking the door. When we peeked over the gate, we didn't see an owner, but we did see two small dogs running around. Although I had to assume the owner was trying to keep the dogs in rather than keep customers out, the message she was sending was just the opposite.

    When we did get inside, one of the dogs jumped on my leg and scratched my leg and pantyhose. The owner's response was a small laugh and a comment about how the dogs thought they owned the store. From all indications, they did.

Chances are those dogs still own the store—if it's still there. I haven't been back.

Whether your prospects' first impression of your business is via a storefront, a phone encounter, or a website, make sure that that first impression lets the prospect know he or she is your business's highest priority.

15. Be Known for Something More Than Doing Business
Start a foundation, get involved in your community, or sponsor an event. This is not only good for you and the world around you, it's good business. We are a Toys for Tots sponsor; we have partnered with Dress For Success; and we started our life planning program for women called Single Step Strategies.

We have reaped the rewards of the joy that comes with sharing, seeing how our efforts have benefitted others, and the advantage of our clients seeing us as having a first-class business. Big businesses promote community projects and support community programs. So should you.

16. Ask for Help
Accepting that you cannot always go it alone qualifies as a sound financial decision. We don't like to ask for help because we don't want to seem needy, but successful people don't go it alone. When we go to work every day, isn't it our job to give help to others? We need to ask as well as give.

Figure out what you know, what you need to know, and what you don't know. Beginning with my disastrous experience hanging wallpaper, I have learned to delegate certain tasks to people who do a good job and whom I can trust to do it well. Being the best you can be means letting others be the best they can be at what they do.

We all need others to inspire us, help us, and enlighten us. For inspiration, read Napoleon Hill's *Think and Grow Rich*, and George Samuel Clason's *The Richest Man in Babylon*. Learn the value of working with coaches and mentors. Build a mastermind group of professionals who are supportive of you and your goals. Having a community of support around you is a priceless asset.

17. Review, Review, Review

Review your progress daily. Review your financials monthly. Review your goals quarterly. Keep track of your sales, your spending, and your earnings. Keep track of the steps necessary to reach your goals.

A good business knows if it is on the winning track because it has the documentation and a tracking system to show where it is and where it is going. A good business maintains a winning strategy. And after all, isn't that why we are in business after all? To win? Vince Lombardi's said it well, "If winning isn't everything, why do they keep score?"

Owning your own business can be a rewarding experience, but it's not a thing to enter into lightly. Use the information in this chapter to develop realistic expectations, plan carefully, and embrace all the tasks associated with ownership. Then follow the basic plan for success: Get in front of more people, more often, and sell more stuff. Repeat, repeat, and repeat.

CHAPTER 7

AND THEN
THERE WAS ONE

When money is plentiful, this is a man's world. When money is scare, it is a woman's world. When all else fails, the woman's instinct comes in. She gets the job done. This is the reason why, in spite of all that happens, we continue to have a world.

~ Ladies Home Journal,
October 1932

CHAPTER 7

AND THEN THERE WAS ONE

BETHANY IS ENTERING a major life change. In her early 60s, she and her husband have recently learned he is facing a serious illness. In the face of this challenge, the couple has chosen to move from their home to an apartment. Bethany jokingly told me she has concluded that she needs to live until age 120. "I have a pile of books I've been planning to read. Unless I live much longer, I won't get to them all."

Books are only one example of the things in life Bethany is sorting through. She is trying to identify the things that are most likely to enhance her next stage of life and hold onto those things, people, and experiences.

After being married for 35 years and raising two children with her husband, Bethany is facing life as a mature single woman. She is creating a plan to ensure that her years alone are as rich and full as possible. Whatever happened in the past, her future is up to her. She is making positive and healthy decisions.

As difficult as the situation is that Bethany is facing, sometimes life sends curve balls that are even more difficult.

Clare lived in a happy relationship with Brad for roughly 30 years. When they began their relationship, Brad was a widow with two young adult children. While they chose to live in separate homes, Clare and Brad shared a life full of intimacy and joy. Clare was involved with Brad's children. As they each neared retirement age, Clare and Brad planned to move in together and build a different sort of life. Unfortunately, Brad became seriously ill before the transition took place.

Accustomed to spending a lot time with Brad, Clare did her best to support him during the early part of his illness. As he became sicker and needed more care, Clare reached out to Brad's children for help, both physically and financially.

The children's perspective was different than Clare's; they expected her to shoulder the entire burden of caring for Brad. The children explained that they had families of their own to support and jobs that took up their time.

Realizing that her own future financial stability was at risk, Clare was faced with a tragic choice. With an unbelievably heavy heart, Clare packed Brad's things and took him to one of the daughter's homes. Then she walked away.

It's hard to imagine that Brad would have wanted this outcome for Clare or himself. Unfortunately, Brad and Clare failed to document their expectations or share them with Brad's daughters. What a difference a plan would have made!

Whether you find yourself alone or with a partner, it's up to you to make decisions about how you want to spend your mature years—and share those decisions with the important people in your life.

It's unwise to just wait and see what happens—with your lifestyle, living situation, or the assets you will pass on to others. The goal is to make the best of your assets (financial, physical, emotional, and relational) while you're still alive.

It all comes down to choices. Things go most smoothly when you make and communicate your choices proactively. But even when life thrusts unhappy situations upon you, you still get to choose how you will react.

Where you are in your life today all comes down to the choices you've already made. Where you will go in life all comes down to the choices that you are going to make.

Begin by making a choice to focus on the future rather than the past. As for me, I never go to high school reunions, because they are all about the past. I can't change the past; I can only make choices about the future. The only thing the past has done has led me to where I am today. I want to spend my energy living fully for today and making plans that ensure I will live fully for the future.

TAKE CONTROL OF YOUR FUTURE

Each of us can learn from the experiences of Bethany and Clare. Statistics tell us that by choice or by chance, life will eventually come down to just us. Eventually, there will be just one. Take control of your future by following these steps:

1. Decide What Kind of Lifestyle You Want
    The following questions will guide you to create a vision of your future:

    - What do you see your golden years looking like? In other words, what do you want from these years? What's your idea of living well in retirement?

    - What are your wishes regarding living arrangements? What's your idea of your forever home?

    - What are your desires surrounding travel?

    - How do you feel about an encore career? Are you looking to continue a professional life, by desire or need? If yes, how would you like your encore career to look? What skills and abilities do you most want to continue contributing in a paid or volunteer position?

    - What activities will bring joy and fulfillment in this phase of life? What kinds of relationships will you have? What avenues will you use to build and maintain social relationships?

    - What will a typical day look like? As you picture an ideal day, are you reading a book, participating in a sport, watching grandkids, working part time, volunteering, or something else?

- What are your values and expectations around what you will do for your children and grandchildren? What are their values and expectations?

- How will you continue to learn and grow throughout your mature years?

- In what ways will you care for your physical health? Will you teach or join a fitness class, walk regularly, or compete in senior-level sports?

2. Do a Formal Retirement Analysis

    Once you have defined your ideal lifestyle, it's time to figure out what you'll need to support that lifestyle. In other words, answer the question: What will it take to fund the life I choose? The following questions can guide you in this analysis:

    - How much money will you need to finance your ideal life?

    - What are your current sources of income? How will those sources change when you retire? For example, what amount can you expect from Social Security? What amount can you draw from investments while still maintaining the principal?

    - How much of a gap is there between the funds needed to support your ideal life and your current finances?

    - If a man has been supporting you, what will happen to your income if that man passes on? (The average age of widowhood is 56.) Do you have insurances to offset such a loss of income?

    - What is the gap, if any, between your estimated income in the face of widowhood and the amount you need to fund your ideal life?

3. Create a Budget to Support the Lifestyle You Choose

    You've dreamt about your ideal retirement. Now it's time to be realistic about preparing to pay for it. As you prepare your budget, be realistic about your income and about how long your savings must last. Consider the following:

- The average lifespan is consistently rising. Twenty years ago, people were expected to retire at 65 and die at 72.

- When Social Security was set up, people were expected to die at 72.

- The average life expectancy for a woman in the U.S. is 79. The average life expectancy for a man is 76. Many people who are now 65 are expected to live to 90 or beyond.

- Older women are twice as likely as older men to be poor.

- Make decisions about what you will do to close any gap. Will you adjust your expectations? Work longer? Delay Social Security? Increase your contributions to a 401K or IRA? Plan an encore career?

4. Prepare Estate-Planning Documents
    Many people assume that if they don't have a sum to leave to their heirs, they don't have an estate. Don't make this mistake. If you own anything, including a house, you have an estate.

    The goal of estate planning is as much about benefitting you as it is benefiting your heirs. The goal is to ensure you make the most of what you have while you arc living, and only then ensuring what's left gets passed on according to your wishes. At a minimum, prepare the following:

- Will

- Financial Power of Attorney

- Medical Power of Attorney

- Family letter

It's not fun to contemplate a time when you might be disabled or unable handle your own affairs, but it is realistic and smart. Unable might be about a serious illness—or even about being temporarily unavailable due to traveling or a short illness. Be sure to have designated someone to take care of your affairs should either be the case. Once you've made the arrangements, the unpleasantness of it is over—and the peace that comes with it remains.

5.   Hold a Family Meeting to Discuss Your End-of-Life Plans

The purpose of a family meeting is to have a two-sided conversation so that no one is caught off guard. In this meeting, you can share your wishes and decisions. Your kids or other significant loved ones can explain how involved they can be.

This meeting, though it may be uncomfortable, is important in heading off a family feud or family breakdown. The tragic situation that Clare found herself in with Brad's children was a full-scale family breakdown. It might have been avoided, or at least minimized, if Brad had held a family meeting with Clare and his children before he became ill.

In my experience, some parents want to use their assets to be generous to their children and some want to punish. Some children have a false sense of entitlement that doesn't align with the parents' choices. In any case, the meeting will clarify the decisions and take away any shock when the parents pass.

If you feel your own family meeting will be difficult or spiral out of control, bring in a third objective party, such as a lawyer or financial planner.

While family meetings can be stressful, they can also draw a family together in love and support. You may remember the story I told earlier in the book about such a meeting. The parents, having decided to pass their wealth to their children while still living, called a family meeting. When the children heard their parents' plan, they asked for an adjustment. The children asked their parents to put the money in long-term health insurance so that everyone could be at peace knowing the parents would be well cared for in any circumstances. What a lovely outcome!

6. Get Help to Put All These Decisions into Action

If this list of steps feels overwhelming to you, don't despair. You don't have to figure it out all at once. And you don't have to do it all on your own. The longer I live, the more I realize that maturity manifests itself in knowing when to ask for help. While I consider myself independent and self-reliant, I've reached out many times for help. Sometimes the person who helped me was a complete stranger.

Most strangers and professionals are eager to help and will treat you fairly. Of course, a small group of less-than-ethical folks are out there too—but you can take steps to protect yourself. One time, some years ago, I walked into my dining room to find that the chandelier was pulling away from the ceiling. I was afraid it would come crashing to the floor.

Wanting to handle the problem quickly, and not having a working relationship with an electrician, I thumbed through the Yellow Pages. The first and biggest ad promised same day service. Without hesitation, I called. The company sent a technician right away.

As soon as the technician entered the door, he asked for a credit card to bill for the initial service fee, promising to deduct the fee from the total cost of the repair. Payment had to be by credit card rather than check.

At this point, the technician hadn't even looked at the light fixture. Intelligent as I am, I somehow was not suspicious at the request. I guess I was too anxious to get past the danger of a crashing chandelier.

When the technician finally examined the chandelier, he quoted an outlandish price. In fact, the price was higher than the original cost of the chandelier. When I complained, the technician simply headed to the door, saying my credit card would be charged for his initial service fee and travel time.

Quickly, I came to my senses and saw this as the scam it was. I told the technician that I would report him to the Attorney General's Office if he charged my card. He countered by saying that if I paid his fee in cash, he would tear up the credit card receipt and fix the light. Wow, I had been conned. But I went along with the deal because I was now "between a rock and a hard place."

After the technician fixed the light and left, I called the Better Business Bureau (BBB) and the Attorney General's Office, as the image of little old ladies being ripped off by this predator company wouldn't go away. Not surprisingly, I found that both organizations had received numerous complaints about this company. Why had I waited until I had an emergency before scouting out a reliable electrician? If I hadn't been in such frenzy, I would have vetted the company before I handed over my credit card. I share this story to remind you as well as myself that we don't make the best decisions when we are under stress.

Most of the stress we experience comes from the unexpected, the unplanned for, and what we consider an emergency. When we find ourselves in an emergency and don't know what steps to take or who to call, we make mistakes. Sometimes those mistakes cost a great deal of money. Don't make an unnecessary mistake with the money that will fund your retirement.

After my experience with the electrical company, I decided never to fall victim to a similar con. I decided to create my own "yellow pages" directory. I made a list of the professionals I might need, including an electrician, plumber, lawyer, and more. I spent the next few months asking friends, family, and business associates whom they used. I checked each referral with the BBB. Then I called each provider and talked to him or her personally to introduce myself.

CHAPTER 8

ONCE UPON A TIME

One of the most courageous things you can do is identify yourself, know who you are, what you believe in and where you want to go

~ Sheila Murray Bethel

CHAPTER 8

ONCE UPON A TIME

WHEN I WAS a young girl, my mother had two songs that were very special to her: "Are You Lonesome Tonight?" by Elvis Presley and "Someone to Watch over Me" by Ella Fitzgerald.

I saw no significance in those songs, until in later years I realized that my mother lived the life I was eventually destined to live—that of a woman with sole responsibility for herself and her family.

My father died when I was four years old, leaving my mother to raise my brother and me on her own. She had not worked outside of the home since we were born, and although my mom had job skills, they were rusty. But she knew that she needed to get up, get dressed up, and get going. Off she went to build a life for herself and her children. My mother's positive attitude about life kept us all going.

When I was in my teens, my mom remarried. That marriage was short-lived and ended in divorce. Once again, her independent spirit and love of life moved her forward. She worked into her 70s at a job she loved. My mother retired, and then took classes at the community college in everything from calligraphy to guitar to literature. She traveled. She entertained. She was the quintessential grandma. She enjoyed every moment of her life, and I learned so much from her. Because of my mother, I knew I had to get up, get dressed up, and get going when my first husband died at age 25. She had modeled this behavior and taught me well.

Still, throughout those years that my mom was single, I am sure she was at times lonesome for companionship beyond friends and family. I am sure she often wished that there was someone who was taking care of her and watching over her.

After the death of my husband, it was a long time before I thought about having a long-term relationship. This is probably why, like my mom, I didn't remarry until my son was in his teens. And then, after my divorce, the thought of another relationship was so unimportant. But there were times when I would wish there was someone who would take care of me, watch over me. I came to understand why those songs were special to my mother.

Then, just as I was focused on my life, my career, and my family, Tom appeared. Nature hates a vacuum, and I had an empty space waiting to be filled by Tom. For the last 18 years, Tom has been my best friend, companion, and significant other. He does watch over me. He does take care of me.

Even so, Tom and I lead separate lives together. He has a cabin in the mountains; I have a carriage home in the suburbs. He loves to golf, while the idea of spending five hours doing one thing that requires that I wait and take my turn is just too much for me. So Tom golfs and I spa. He sings, directs a barbershop chorus, and teaches music. I love music, but the rule in my family is that I am not allowed to sing unless at least 10 other people are singing at the same time; and then I have to sing quietly. Tom shops and cooks. I break out in a cold sweat if I have to go to WalMart. I get lost in the grocery store, and cooking is a necessity only if Tom is not there to cook for me.

I work a lot; Tom works a little. I like HGTV. He likes sports. I have a gym membership; he has Steeler season tickets. He has his money, his income. I have mine.

Tom and I are and will remain independent.

But Tom and I love to go the theater together. We like musicals, and we enjoy discussing current events. We have the same philosophies about life and the world at large. We enjoy dinners at five-star restaurants. Tom and I travel a lot, and we are great traveling companions. We have shared adventures such as ballooning, flying lessons, segwaying, ziplining, hiking on glaciers in Alaska, and many more. We work on the *New York Times'* crossword puzzles together in ink. We like dark meat chicken, dark chocolate, and any kind of seafood. We raise a beagle. We share house responsibilities. We never discuss money or who is paying for what. One or the other of us just takes care of the bill. We have a joint travel account.

Tom and I are and plan to remain together.

I am often asked if I would have wanted to meet Tom when he and I were much younger so that we could have enjoyed our relationship for most of our lives. The fact is that Tom and I were not the same people when we were much younger. We would not have been ready for the relationship we currently have. The challenges, changes, and circumstance that brought us to where we are today made us the people we are today—ready for our life together.

Today, Tom and I are planning not to leave each other by choice, but we know one of us will leave by chance, and we are prepared. We have prepared our "bucket list," completed our estate planning, and made our final arrangements. We have discussed health care arrangements. We have talked to our family members. And although our plan is to go from our house to God's house when the time comes, we assume one of us will go first, preparing the way for the other.

In the meantime, Tom and I seize each day. We get up, get dressed up ,and get going. And we are grateful.

You might say that I've spent the last 18 years with my version of Prince Charming, but Tom never was—and still is not— my plan. Long before Tom entered my life, I learned that I am not Cinderella, and that I don't need a man to be my savior. I'm CEO of my own life and I don't need someone else to live a rich and full life. I don't underestimate the richness and fullness Tom adds to my life, but he is not the sole source of these things for me. Nor me for him.

Over the last 18 years, as in all the years since my husband died, my passion for independence for women has never faltered. While my daily work focuses on finances, experience tells me that financial independence is but one aspect of a complete whole. Any woman's financial independence is inextricably linked to how she manages so many other aspects of her life—areas like relationships, health, and business—especially during times of change or transition.

You have learned that statistics indicate that you will be alone and responsible for yourself for at least some portion of your life. Maybe you are in such a time now.

Whatever your status, take the next step toward a healthy independence. I am convinced that the most important step is deciding that no matter where you are in life, whether in early, middle, or later years, you need to take charge of your own life and live abundantly.

I encourage you to create your own definition of abundance by finding your purpose and living into it. Embrace the fact that you are a person of worth with unique contributions to make to the world. Figure out what gives you satisfaction, energy, and joy, and build those things into your life.

Create a vision for your ideal life and then develop a budget to show yourself what you'll need to support that life. Set goals every quarter, or at least every year, to get you where you want to go. Life changes as you navigate various seasons, such as childrearing, empty nesting, and retirement. Regularly take a step back to assess and change as your life changes.

Pursue some short-term and some longer-term goals. For example, you might choose to cut back on luxuries for the short term so you can afford a special vacation this year. For the long-term, you may need education or a certification to get the job of your dreams. If so, make a long-term plan set goals to accomplish them in manageable steps, even if it takes longer than you wish to get there.

Don't forget to make one of your goals to build a stash of cash, and don't forget to invest in your own health. Cash and health are key ingredients of a woman's independence.

Embrace your ability to vacuum out relationships as well as anything that doesn't serve you. You have the power and the responsibility, to yourself, to get rid of the parade-rainers who hold you back from your dreams. Evaluate your relationships and remove yourself from any toxic ones. While this may be scary, you won't be able to build healthy relationships if toxic ones are taking up all the space. Remember, two things cannot occupy the same space at the same time. It's a scientific impossibility.

The same principle is true for stuff. If you are consuming money and energy to buy and maintain stuff that is crowding your life, take an inventory and let some go. You'll have more money and energy for important things, such as meeting your goals.

As you step into abundance, seek out what you need from multiple sources. If you have a man in your life, don't expect him to meet all your needs. Such a man is the stuff of fairy tales, not real life. Pursue friendships as a vital part of your healthy life, and learn to embrace some time alone as well. Alone is not the same as lonely.

No matter what your age or level of independence, you will always need help. It's healthy to embrace this, and even to embrace the fact that you'll need help from strangers. Perhaps the person who most impressed this truth upon me is a little girl named Alex.

Once upon a time, a little girl named Alex believed she was a princess. She was known to one and all as Princess Alex. As Alex is my great niece, I was honored to buy into her fantasy of being Her Royal Highness. Alex's family and friends can't quite remember how Alex took on the title, but somewhere around the time Alex learned to talk, she began to refer to herself that way. She then had expectations that she be treated like a princess, and it was easy for the people in her life to live up to her expectations, since Alex was a sweet and beautiful little girl.

Alex's parents decorated her room like a castle, and family members bought her clothes fit for a little princess. She had princess paraphernalia and even a tiara for special occasions.

When she was 5 years old, I took Princess Alex to a downtown department store for Christmas story time with the Berenstain Bears. That day, Alex was dressed in pink lace with a white fur coat and a white fur muff, as any little princess should be.

Because we all know that bears cannot read, Alex wondered who would be doing the reading. As we waited, a young woman, beautifully dressed as a princess, walked into the room to read the story. She referred to herself as Princess Anne. As Alex was in awe, she moved to the front of the room to get a closer look. She listened intently to the story, and her eyes never left the princess.

When Princess Anne finished reading, she announced that all of the children would be able to get their picture taken with the Berenstain Bears and that they should form a line. As Alex and I waited, she turned to me and said, "Mannie, I don't want my picture taken with the bears. I want it taken with the princess."

I approached the photographer and I told him of Alex's request. The photographer said that he was sorry but that he was to take pictures only of the children with the bears.

Alex slowly hung her head and looked a bit sad but very intent. Suddenly, she turned around, let go of my hand, and walked directly up to the Princess. Alex said, "Princess Anne, I would like to get my picture taken with you; after all, I am a princess, too. I am Princess Alex."

The young woman smiled at Alex as she answered, "Princess Alex, I am so sorry I didn't recognize you. Well, of course, you will have your picture taken with me." And so she did.

I was reminded of some good life lessons that day. Alex knew who she was. She was confident and happy with herself. She believed in herself and her dreams. No one would deter her from her path.

How many times have we let others dictate who we are? How many times have we let others lead us down their path because of our lack of confidence to proceed on our own life's journey?

Alex needed help she knew to ask for it. How often have we needed or wanted things and have forgotten to ask for help?

Although Alex knew I would do anything to make her happy, she quickly discovered that I was not the person with the ability to get her the help she needed in this instance. So she went to the source. How many times when we finally ask for help, do we discover that those we have asked are not necessarily the source of all we need?

Who is the source of what you need in your life? For some of us, the source is friends and family; for some of us the source is an institution of higher learning, business contacts, or the community we live in. Or it is the Ultimate Source of all good things, a Higher Power.

If life isn't giving you all that you want, maybe, like Princess Alex, you need to believe in yourself, step out of line, ask for help, and go to your source. Imagine, then, how abundant your life could be when *you* are the plan.

ABOUT THE AUTHOR

ABOUT THE AUTHOR

FOR OVER 35 YEARS, Mary Grace Musuneggi has been helping women to develop clear strategies for pursuing their financial goals. Chairman & CEO of The Musuneggi Financial Group, Mary Grace recently launched the Starting Out/Starting Over program for women who are hitting the "Start" or "Reset" buttons: new graduates, new mothers and grandmothers, new business owners, women transitioning into a second or even a third career, and women who are navigating divorce or finding themselves single—by choice or by chance.

Throughout her career, Mary Grace has often met women who were facing challenges that dramatically influenced the quality of their lives. Having already experienced life from so many perspectives—from single to married to widowed; from stay-at-home mom to working, single parent; from trailblazer for women in her industry to an award-winning CEO—Mary Grace knows how to handle life's curveballs and make her own personal happiness and professional success. Two rules have held true for her throughout her journey: Find and use resources wisely, and have the courage to take the first step.

Single Step Strategies, an educational resource for women in Western PA, was born out of Mary Grace's desire to share this and more in a format that is be easily accessible to all women who are ready to take their first step toward success, happiness, and independence. For over 10 years, Single Step Strategies has been bridging the gaps between women facing a challenging situation, the resources they need, and their goals.

Mary Grace is also the author of *Single Steps: Strategies for Abundant Living.* She frequently speaks to women's organizations about financial planning and lifestyle issues.